THE WORLD OF
GOLF
COLLECTABLES

>>>>>>>>>><<<<<<<<<

THE WORLD OF
GOLF
COLLECTABLES

Sarah Fabian Baddiel

FOREWORD BY PETER DOBEREINER

WELLFLEET
PRESS

DEDICATION

I dedicate this book to Joe Murdoch and Bob Kuntz for their warm friendship and support to me. Without them, Golf Collecting would not exist! And to my "lofted" club.

ACKNOWLEDGEMENTS

I would like to thank Karen Bednarski and Andy Mutch of the United States Golf Association, Far Hills, New Jersey, and David Berkowitz of Golf's Golden Years, 2929 N. Western Avenue, Chicago, Illinois 60618, for their tremendous assistance, advice and support whilst I was researching and photographing my book. They allowed me a completely free rein with their collections for several days while I took over part of their premises as a studio. Without their help, I would not have been able to write this book. I would also like to thank Bill Burnett and Patty Carroll, who took the photographs. Acknowledgements must go to Ben Crenshaw from Grand Slam for the facts about Bobby Jones, and to Allick A. Watt and Ms Liz Pook for their help and support.

The World of Golf Collectables
First published in 1992 by Wellfleet Books
an imprint of Book Sales, Inc.
110 Enterprise Avenue
Secaucus, New Jersey 07094

ISBN 1-55521-746-X

Printed and bound in Singapore

CONTENTS

FOREWORD

Take it from me. I am a pro and know about golf books. When you buy a book, or are given one, there is an implied suggestion that the book is to be read. The implication is particularly strong in the case of a novel. And if the author happens to be Mr Evelyn Waugh or Count Leo Tolstoy then the act of reading it can be an enjoyable and enriching experience, maybe even more so than devoting an equivalent amount of time to watching soap operas.

Golf books are quite another matter. Most of them are not for reading, goodness me no. Their purpose, their very raison d'etre, is to be given away as presents. We can go further and break golf books down into their specialized categories and functions.

GOLF BIOGRAPHIES. These are written by impoverished hacks, known in the trade as ghosts, and are intended to show the subject in a favourable light. They either ignore or totally misrepresent unsavoury episodes in the famous golfer's life so are best classified as fiction when being put away unread in the bookcase.

CLUB HISTORIES. This is a form of vanity publishing, usually the work of a retired member with nothing better to do with his time. They mainly consist of lists of past captions and recitations of the dreary virtues of some long serving club professional. Theoretically they could be read but they are so boring as to be unreadable.

ANTHOLOGIES. This is known as the bubble and squeak syndrome, a rehash of yesterday's leftovers, the last resort of an illiterate editor trying to fend off the bailiffs by reprinting articles, mostly written by me and reproduced without permission or recompense.

INSTRUCTION. The only known value of books on golf instruction is to practise your swing while balancing one of them on top of your head.

STOCKING FILLERS. Collections of extremely feeble golf jokes allegedly written by TV personalities. Best posted well before Christmas so that the recipient has time to fob it off as a present on somebody he dislikes.

COFFEE TABLE. Until quite recently the function of this genre was self-explanatory. These books are traditionally intended as domestic decor, like curtains and throw cushions, to be left around on occasional tables in order to create an illusion of culture. But now that dratted woman Sarah Baddiel has kicked that convention out of the window. She did a coffee table book, 'Golf. The Golden Years', and filled it with fascinating pictures. Worse, she completely and, I suspect, deliberately travestied the purpose of text, which is to provide a soft, grey background for the illustrations, and wrote interesting words. It sold in thousands. People read it! With pleasure! They clamoured for more. And now she has produced this sequel. It is, if anything, even better. Golf publishing will never be the same again.

PETER DOBEREINER

Opposite: Open Championship golf game, by Beacon Hudson of Boston, Massachusetts, 1925.

INTRODUCTION

The game of golf as we know it today was first played in Scotland sometime before 1457, but other ball and stick games had been played for centuries before. In the Roman Empire, for example, a game called *paganica* was played with a feather-packed ball and a stick. By the fourteenth century, a variety of golf-like games were being played, including *Kolven's colf* in Holland, *chole* and *jeu de mail* in Belgium and northern France, and hurley or shinty in Ireland.

One of the favourite items in the history of the game is the fact, as everybody knows, that in 1592 and 1593 the Town Council of Edinburgh forbade the amusement on Sundays. This restriction Mr Andrew Lang has commented upon with frank regret. He mentions as "early martyrs" those who were prosecuted for playing "gowff on the Links of Leith every Sabbath the time of the sermonses." At Perth another "martyr" suffered in the same cause in 1604. In 1603 James VI appointed one, William Mayne, to be Royal club maker, and in 1618 he gave James Melvill a monopoly of ball-making at four shillings each ball. These are interesting particulars, both "Royal" and "Ancient." Hitherto Dornoch has had no such story to tell. I have, however, just perused satisfactory evidence that golf was played in the vicinity of the county town of Sutherland as early as 1617. We know that golf had reached the Orkneys as early as 1585, and the "golf-stream" may, for aught we know, have flowed across the Pentland Firth and come south *via* Dornoch. At any rate, the

J. C. Barclay (1876–1923), signed artist's proof of etching of *The Royal and Ancient Club House, c.* 1910.

Open Championship Programme, Royal Lytham and St. Anne's, 1926.

following entry from "Tutour Accompt-bookes" of Sir Robert Gordon, curator for his nephew, John, Earl of Sutherland, is well authenticated:–

Discharge of Silver (1617)

"Item of twelf pounds this yeir given to my Lords for bowes, arrowes, golff clubbs and balles, bookes, paper, and other necessaries for his exercises."

The MS. from which this entry was copied is in the ducal castle at Dunrobin, and it may be mentioned that the particular Earl referred to was he who afterwards became the Covenanter, and who was born in 1609 and died in 1679. He was, therefore, but eight years old when he swung his short club above the grass – and no doubt sometimes under it – on the fresh downs that skirt in ample acreage the little but Royal Burgh of Dornoch.

It was the Scots who evolved the basic features of modern golf: balls were hit across country to a hole in the ground, without interference from an opponent. In 1754 the Royal and Ancient Golf Club, St Andrews, was founded. The club had a very important influence on the game and remains the ruling body to this day. It decreed, among other things, that a course should have eighteen holes. Meanwhile, in England, the Royal Blackheath Golf Club had been established in 1607, possibly through the activities of Mary Queen of Scots and her son James I of England, who were both good players. James's son Henry played on common land in Greenwich, and this area was to become Royal Blackheath.

In the early days the game was mostly confined to the rich because of the cost of feathery golf balls. These were made of boiled goose feathers stuffed into leather and were hand-sewn. Often the ball cost four times as much as the clubs. The gutta percha ball was evolved in 1848. Since gutta percha is very hard-wearing and the balls were cheaper to produce, golf now became accessible to the middle classes, who had more money and more free time at their disposal. By 1870 there were thirty golf clubs in Britain, by 1890 three hundred, and by 1905 three thousand.

London has become a much more tolerable and reasonable place to live in since its suburban wild places have turned themselves into golf courses – links we like to call them, but of course "links" ought properly to be the name of that sandy-soiled ground by the sea, the creation of alluvial deposit, which we do not get about London. The nearest in approach to it, in manner of formation, are the two links at Richmond, the course of the Mid-Surrey Club close to the station and that of the Richmond Golf Club, in Sudbrook Park. Here the formation evidently is due to a silting up by the river, but the result is a soil a good deal richer, and a grass a good deal more generous, than we find on the real sandy links beside the sea, where all is ideal for golf. But, though we cannot realise the seaside ideal inland, we have, nevertheless, a great deal to be thankful for, and I do not think we ever can recognize how much we in the Great City owe now to the golf that is around it until we try to picture what our life would be without the golf. And yet it is very few years since the golf within the reach of the Londoner was confined to two greens, the classical

THE LONDONER AND HIS GOLF by Horace G. Hutchinson, from *The House Annual*, 1902

A hand-painted MacIntyre Burslem teapot, registration number 291478, 4¼ inches tall, *c.* 1898. This factory became the Moorcroft factory.

Blackheath and the more modern Wimbledon. Within twenty years, within fifteen, and even within ten, the change in the face of Nature about London, as we see it when we travel out by train, is wonderful enough. To be sure, it may be said that in those by-gone years we did not want golf, that the supply has sprung up to satisfy the demand, and that the demand was sufficiently supplied by the Blackheath and Wimbledon Greens of the period before the big "boom." That is quite true, but the fact that so many Londoners did not know what possibilities they were missing does not alter the fact that they are a deal healthier and happier now from having recognized, better late than never, those possibilities.

There are many good Metropolitan courses that it is impossible even to mention, for the lack of space, and to them all apology is due for the sin of omission. After all, when you come to an hour's journey by rail, and to see something further at the end of that, by motor or by horse-drawn vehicle, then it becomes a question whether the more blessed thing to do is not to sit tight in the train till you get to the actual links – to the seaside. It does not take so much more time or toil to get to Sandwich, let us say. To be sure it may be objected that here, too, there is a distance to drive – not a long distance, but it all means time and money – before you are on the tee. So shall we suggest Littlestone, instead? For you may live there right on the tee, even as you do at St. Andrews or North Berwick. That is the peculiar blessedness of so many of these Scottish greens – take the two named above, or Prestwick, or Carnoustie or Elie, the names occur to one by the score – that you live, and eat your breakfast, right down on the course. There is no worry of catching trains or jolting up your works in cabs rattling on country roads before you begin the delicate business of golf, which needs all nerves and works to be in such perfect order. So that, after all, it becomes a further question whether it is not quite as pleasant to take a night train up to one of these Scottish greens, to breakfast close beside the tee, after dining in London and in comfort, and stroll forth in the morning like a gentleman of leisure instead of like a bagman snatching an hour or two between two trains.

Of course, a man cannot altogether pick and choose his club. Most of the popular clubs in the neighbourhood of London have a long waiting list, and the new candidate's name has to be inscribed at the tail of it. But some of the best greens and

Penfold Pro-shop poster, "He played a Penfold", 9 × 15 inches, *c.* 1950.

Left to right: 18 ct gold medal with crossed clubs, no inscription; Neasden Golf Club medal won by Garden G. Smith, May 1896. The medallion is suspended from a silver and gold transitional headed wood and a cleek with a "gutty" ball; A silver and enamel Monthly Medal, February 1912. Won by H. Hambleton 65 − 10 = 55.

H. M. Williamson and Sons sandwich platter, 8 × 12 inches, depicting golfers of the period in natural colours, *c.* 1912. The coffee-size jug and sugar bowl are 2 inches high. Among the golfers shown are Harry Vardon, James Braid, John Henry Taylor and a group of caddies.

some of the classic courses afar off, St. Andrews and North Berwick, and many more, are open to all comers who will pay a small green fee. To be sure, going to a distant land without the certainty of finding a friend is a forlorn hope – play with the local professional may be improving, but is apt to grow wearisome – and on these pilgrimages the golfer is well advised if he take some friend, his equal, more or less, at golf, with him. No doubt it is a risky experiment, it is straining the bonds of friendship hard, you may lose friend, temper, money, and many balls, even Haskells; but "you must take some risks, even at this game," as the old gentleman said cheerily when expostulated with for driving into people at short range.

The first British Championship was played at Prestwick in 1860 when eight professionals competed for the Challenge Belt. In 1861 the British Open began, and both professionals and amateurs were allowed to enter. In 1863 the prize money for the winner was £5, but by 1880 this had risen to £20, and by 1900 to £100. The early professionals also took bets, gave lessons, and made and sold clubs in order to finance their way of life.

In the earlier days of Golf, although there was a recognized champion, there was no accompanying symbol of supremacy by which he who claimed the title could substantiate his right to it. Allan Robertson was, without doubt, the greatest golfer of his age – a veritable champion amongst champions – yet there was never vouchsafed to him, as proof of his prowess, either cup or belt. It was not until 1860 that a champion trophy was forthcoming. In that year the Prestwick Golf Club presented a "Challenge Belt," to be competed for on their own green annually, and to become the property of anyone winning it three times in succession. Between the

HISTORY OF THE GOLFING CHAMPIONSHIP by C. Robertson Bauchope, from *Golfing Annual*, Vol I, 1888

Clubs. (From bottom to top): Duplex,
Standard Golf Co., Mills, RL 24 model;
giant niblick, Tom Stewart, c.1910;
Walter Hagen concave wedge, c.1920;
early putt-shaped niblick, no mark,
c.1890.

year of its institution and 1867, old Tom Morris had won it four times, and Willie Park three, but as neither had done so consecutively the gift still stood its ground. But about the latter date a new star rose in the golfing firmament – one before which all others had to pale their ineffectual fires. This was young Tom Morris, who soon proved himself quite a royal and ancient Samson by metaphorically standing head and shoulders above his compeers of the green. This nonpareil, as is well-known, by scoring his third successive victory in 1870 transferred the champion belt for good to his own keeping. For some time thereafter it appeared as if a fresh badge of supremacy would not be provided, but the various golfing combinations throughout the country put their shoulders to the wheel, and the present Champion Cup was duly announced for open competition in 1872. The conditions attached to it differ materially from those associated with its predecessor. The Cup cannot pass into the permanent possession of any player, and instead of one green being the scene of the annual conflict, Prestwick, St. Andrews, and Musselburgh have to be visited each year in turn. That the latter proviso is an improvement is self-evident, and that the former is a good saving clause has already more than once been experienced; for, although Jamie Anderson, of St. Andrews, was successful in 1877, '78 and '79; and Bob Ferguson, of Musselburgh, in 1880, '81, and '82, the Cup is still to the fore. One important point in connection with it cannot be overlooked. It differs from all other challenge prizes in that it can be contested by both amateurs and professionals, and in these days of exclusiveness this fact in itself is sufficiently rare to be remarkable.

With the advent of the gutta percha ball and, after 1899, of the rubber-core ball, which was often called the Haskell after the man who invented it, a new era had begun. Clubs underwent less rapid changes, but by the early 1920s they were factory-produced and less expensive. Even so a few club-makers continued to handcraft clubs during this time.

From those days until the present time nearly every resort prospectus, newspaper and magazine advertisement has featured the golf courses almost as prominently as the hotel. But the one-time makeshift hotel links will not fool the golfer of 1921. The players refuse to tolerate poor play grounds. The modern golfer is fastidious and he insists on modern golf conditions. If he happens to be attracted by a misleading advertisement and arrives only to find a slovenly collection of featureless, ill-conditioned holes, does he endure it patiently as of old? Not much! He is not

GOLF THE MAGNET by A.W. Tillinghurst, from *Golf Illustrated*, January 1921

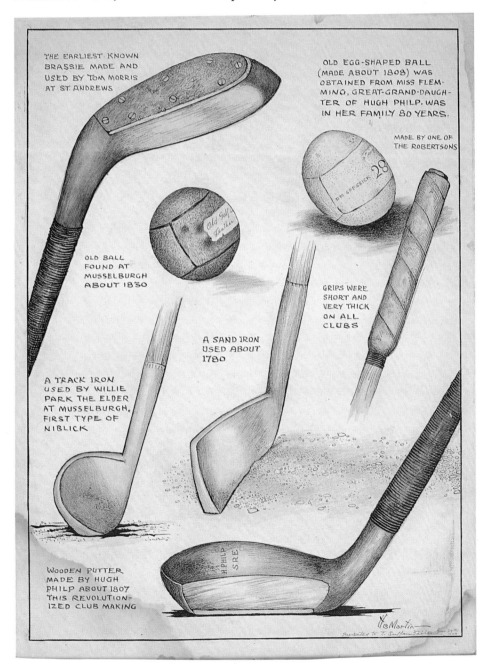

THE EARLIEST KNOWN BRASSIE MADE AND USED BY TOM MORRIS AT ST. ANDREWS

OLD EGG-SHAPED BALL (MADE ABOUT 1808) WAS OBTAINED FROM MISS FLEMMING, GREAT-GRAND-DAUGHTER OF HUGH PHILP. WAS IN HER FAMILY 80 YEARS.

MADE BY ONE OF THE ROBERTSONS

OLD BALL FOUND AT MUSSELBURGH ABOUT 1830

GRIPS WERE SHORT AND VERY THICK ON ALL CLUBS

A SAND IRON USED ABOUT 1780

A TRACK IRON USED BY WILLIE PARK THE ELDER AT MUSSELBURGH. FIRST TYPE OF NIBLICK

WOODEN PUTTER MADE BY HUGH PHILP ABOUT 1807 THIS REVOLUTIONIZED CLUB MAKING

H. B. Martin, pen and ink of clubs, putters and balls. The earliest known brassies made and used by Tom Morris at St. Andrews, old egg-shaped ball made about 1808 and obtained from Miss Fleming, great grand-daughter of Hugh Philp. Old ball found at Musselburgh, 1830. Grips were very short and thick on all clubs. Track iron used by Willie Park Senior at Musselburgh. First type of niblick. Sand iron used about 1870. Wooden putter made by Hugh Philp about 1807.

Signed photograph of Tom Morris.

backward in voicing his dissatisfaction nor dilatory in checking out and seeking accommodations at another resort, where the quality of the golf is of established repute. And thereafter he turns loose his batteries of criticism among his friends, which certainly is not beneficial to the future business of the place of disappointment. But so long is the arm of golf that few resorts are without at least one course, and frequently a number. Without these only a corporal's guard could be induced to patronize them.

To their credit be it said that resort courses are surely improving in excellence and many of them are truly great. They have to be thoroughly modern or the many thousands of tourist golfers, who flock to such places and crowd them to capacity, would not wear paths to them – placing them on the map by enthusiastic reports of ideal golf conditions far more effectively than could be accomplished by any amount of glowing description in prospectus form. It is only necessary for resorts to announce the dates of the opening of their courses and tournament schedules, keeping them in the public eye naturally enough, and the golfing public will do the rest. No golf course ever achieved distinction through advertising alone. It had to have true merit to survive the acid test of the discriminating golfer of today.

It can only be a matter of a comparatively short time when every town of any consequence will have at least one course. It is likely that in nine cases out of ten the

growth of the residential section of any town, which has not already developed a very marked expansion in one direction or another, may be absolutely figured to reach out to the golf course. It is so certain that any astute speculator in real estate may well afford to have a proper site for golf selected, secure possession of the tract and much more property in the neighborhood, and actually give the golf land to a desirable coterie of golfers for development and maintenance. It ceases to be speculation because it is so sure, and incidentally tremendously profitable.

Some years ago in Florida a large tract of typical land was purchased at an average price of about fifteen dollars an acre, some of it as low as eight. It was covered with palmetto and for the most part was a jungle. It is six miles out from the nearest town, and ten years ago there were a few scattered bungalows along the line. Today there is a golf course there – with a large hotel, many fine residences, paved streets all the way from the town and a car line direct to the course. The town has stretched out its arm to the golf course in the jungle. Try to buy some of that property for fifteen dollars an acre today. It is running into three figures for bungalow sites. The golf course is becoming a more powerful magnet every day.

Left: A watercolour of Bobby Jones presented to the Club.

Right: Arnold Palmer holding the US Amateur trophy in 1954, USGA Photograph Library.

Left: Dr. W. G. Grace. "Following the ball, the Grand Old Man playing at Maidenhead, April 1909", from *Golfing UK*.

Right: Lee, pen and ink wash for the *Evening News*, 23 February 1946: "Oh dear! Those allotment enthusiasts have started their propaganda again!"

Following the Second World War, golf-course construction boomed, and numbers rose from 4,870 in 1947 to about 15,000 in 1991. Hundreds of thousands of new enthusiasts wanted to play the game. Fans everywhere wanted to see the low-scoring professionals in action. Players of the new era, such as Patty Berg, Ben Hogan, Jack Nicklaus, Arnold Palmer and Babe Zaharias, travelled abroad, while spectators at home followed their matches on television. Tournaments became sporting spectacles of increasing international popularity. The United States Open Golf Championship was televised nationwide in America for the first time in 1954 from Baltusrol Golf Club in Springfield, New Jersey.

Manufacturers now experimented with aluminium and graphite shafts. Inventors created solid balls made of plastics and designed cut-resistant covers for wound balls. The rules governing equipment were refined in order to retain the traditions of the game and a more rigorous testing programme for equipment was instituted. Now, every year more and more people take up golf.

GOLF, A DEFINITION by David Robertson Forgan, from *Memories of the Links*, 1930

It is a science – the study of a lifetime, in which you may exhaust yourself but never your subject. It is a contest, a duel or a mêlée, calling for courage, skill, strategy and self-control. It is a test of temper, a trial of honor, a revealer of character. It affords a chance to play the man, and act the gentleman. It means going into God's out-of-doors, getting close to nature, fresh air, exercise, a sweeping away of the mental cobwebs, genuine re-creation of the tired tissues. It is a cure for care – an antidote to worry. It includes companionship with friends, social intercourse, opportunities for courtesy, kindliness and generosity to an opponent. It promotes not only physical health but moral force.

THE ARCHITECTURE OF GOLF COURSES

No two golf courses are the same, although all are based on the same foundations. The history of golf architecture begins in about 1880. Until then nature had been allowed to reign. Today golf architecture has become big business and many of the great players have become architects.

Had I the pen of Mr. H.G. Wells what visions might I not be able to conjure up of the golf course of the future! I might, for all I know, describe putting greens perched on the top of enormous towers, covered with synthetic turf and controlled by a committee of international experts. I might – but then I have not the pen of that great romantic seer. I must stick to the earth and even so my visions must be of an ignorant and unromantic character.

All golfers, whatever their standard of play, like the best possible surface to play upon. Therefore in looking into the future we need have no fear of a revolution of the rabbits against the tigers on any greenkeeping question. When on the other hand we come to the question of design it is possible to imagine an infuriated eighteen handicap rabble pursuing with execrations tumbrils filled with architects and scratch players. Yet I do not think this will ever happen because the modern architect is coming to be more and more on the side of the "man in the street" golfer. He no longer thinks of punishing the bad shot of the bad player for that can look after itself; he is more and more disposed to make difficulties for the good player's good

THE GOLF COURSE OF THE FUTURE by Bernard Darwin, from the *Journal of the Board of Greenkeeping Research*, Vol II, no. 6, Spring 1932

Postcards. (From left to right): the Links, Gullane, after a painting by P. Phillmore, 1909; Golf Club House, Elie, 1914; Home Green, Royal and Ancient Golf Club House, Cyril Tolley putting, 1916; the first tee, Gullane, 1906.

shot which is yet not quite good enough. Once upon a time, in the days of ramparts stretched across the fairway, the poor rabbit had often to do a very dull thing; he had to take an iron and play short. To-day he will not get up in two, but there is a way open to him by which he can get as far as he is able. It may almost be said that there has been a peaceful revolution and owing to this gradual and imperceptible democratisation of the game there will never be any real revolution at all. I do, however, look forward to one change. I hope for at least two sets of teeing grounds to be in regular every-day use. To-day there are often in fact front tees and back tees in commission and the front tees make a better and pleasanter game for the average player, the back tees for the young slasher. At present the average player will not recognize this because he scents some subtle affront to his vanity. So he spoils his own fun by going too far back and at the same time abuses architects or committees for making the course too long. I cannot believe that he will always be so exceedingly silly and I look forward to a time when two and even three sets of tees are in regular use and the player almost automatically chooses those best suited to his powers and his enjoyment.

The architect will go as far as possible more and more back to nature and make less and less use of his spade for digging bunkers. When the great golf boom began in the eighties and nineties those who made the new courses were, as it seems, for the most part quite incapable of analyzing the merits of the old ones. They had a magnificient model which they all admired in St. Andrews but they did not perceive that the merit of this enormously great course lay not in its bunkers but in the slight rises and falls and turns and twists in the ground. So beyond occasionally putting a green in the bottom of a deep dell they did not use their ground to the best advantage

ome Green, Royal and Ancient Golf Club House, (Cyril Tolley Putting) St. Andrews

The First Tee
M. Wane & Co., Edinbro'.

Gullane

and disfigured it by hideous ramparts and rule of thumb bunkers. Their successors have exactly reversed the procedure. Whenever it is at all possible they have made every possible use of the natural rise and fall of the ground. Moreover when nature has done nothing to help and they have had to be artificial their artifice has not taken the form of bunkers but of altering the lie of the land. Sometimes they can do wonderful things with "scoops" which their predecessors could not, and my impression is that they will do more and more in this direction; they will not make a flat piece of ground into a mine field of bunkers, but they will make it rise and fall in interesting undulations. The classic example of what can be done still remains, I suppose, the Lido course in America where great engines sucked the sand out of the sea, spread it like so much jam in artistic curves on a dead flat surface and produced a splendid sea-side course on the top of a dull swamp. That was of course a colossal undertaking beyond the reach of ordinary mortals but on a smaller scale this titivating of the face of nature can be done. The golfing architect is becoming more of a landscape gardener and less of a mere ruthless ruffian with a shovel.

I hope but I am not sure that the era is past in which golfers talked over much of the "fairness" and "unfairness" of holes and courses. There was a time when people thought that the player should always in all possible circumstances be allowed a full bang from the tee and that it was a gross injustice if his ball, when fairly struck, went into a bunker. To-day I trust that the modern architect has taught them that this is not so; that the golfer must use his own head as well as that of his club, and that it is good fun and true sport to have to think before playing the shot. I believe that some of the most interesting and exacting holes in the world might be devised which would insist on a mashie shot from the tee and a full brassey shot for the second. I

21

HISTORICAL
BRITISH AND
AMERICAN
COURSES:
PRESTWICK by
George W.
Greenwood, from
*The American
Golfer*, March 1930

Original poster for the Scarborough Golf
Club. A foursome competition held in
1899 between F. G. Tait, W. Park, J. Ball
and H. Vardon.

cannot see why some genius of an architect should not devise such holes. Moreover, since we are told that the brassey is becoming atrophied, because golfers hit their tee shots so far, here is a method of restoring the lost glory of that glorious club. Perhaps we are not yet educated up to that pitch but we may become so. There is no valid reason why the drive should always come first and the iron shot next. Obviously we must end with the putting, but apart from that the greater variety the better. One of the most entertaining holes I ever saw could hardly be reached with two full wooden club shots, but could be comfortably reached with a mashie and an iron. There is a puzzle for the reader to think out for himself.

Various factors will affect the layout of the course, including the existing lie of the land, the required length for each hole, the positioning of the bunkers and water hazards, and the dimension of the green in proportion to the yardage of the hole.

Every golf course, like most human beings, has a personality. This aphorism is certainly true of Prestwick, an important link in a great chain of perfectly natural courses stretching for fifty miles, or so, along the shores of the beautiful Firth of Clyde, and down the west coast of Scotland. In age and tradition Prestwick is a close rival of St. Andrews. For eleven years from 1860 to 1870, the Championship Belt, a massive silver contrivance, which the reigning champion had the right of wearing round his waist, was played for at Prestwick.

It is true of St. Andrews that those who go there for the first time do so in a state of awe, for it is here that mighty people sit in state making laws and issuing edicts to be obeyed by golfers in the uttermost parts of the earth. There is not quite the same feeling of awe and veneration when one goes to Prestwick, though, to be sure, it is a place which one approaches respectfully, and with due regard for its history, dating back beyond the recollection of living man.

It was not so long ago that members of this golfing fastness were in the habit of putting their sons' names down for membership the day they were born, and even so they had to wait twenty years before they got in. At the present time, you wait twelve to fifteen years before election, the persons nominated in 1918 when the Great War came to an end are now being admitted to the club. This will convey an idea of the exclusiveness and the position which Prestwick holds in the world of golf.

Now as to the links itself, one of the most difficult in Scotland, and in the minds of a great many people ranking higher than St. Andrews. Personally, I do not share this view, because it is just as absurd to attempt a comparison between Prestwick and St. Andrews, as it is to try and compare Garden City with Pine Valley. For example, St. Andrews is flat with wide spaces in which to drive, while Prestwick is a links of towering and majestic sandhills on which grow a species of sea grass two feet high, with stems as stout and as prickly as darning-needles.

Between the hills are little valleys of glorious seaside turf, and running through the course are the swift waters of the notorious Pow Burn, which has been the watery grave of many a celebrated golfer. Such fearsome names as the "Himalayas" and the "Alps" suggest tremendous carries over mountains of sand and broken country; imagination is translated into fact when you get to Prestwick.

Handcut wooden puzzle of Michael Brown's Life Association calendar of Prestwick Himalaya Hole, *c.* 1914. In the picture are J. H. Taylor, George Duncan, James Braid and Harry Vardon.

An inland course will obviously be very different from a links on the seashore, especially one in Scotland. The wind conditions will also have to be taken into account and an effort will be made to ensure that the player has the wind behind him for a number of holes and then has to play into it. The course should be designed as a test of the players' ability, demanding a variety of shots in every game.

In writing of the ideal golf course one must begin with certain assumptions. One must assume, for instance, that for the lover of this sport the ideal course will never lose its charm; that it will always present to him interesting problems; and that his delight in it will increase no matter how often nor for how many years he plays it. We must assume that it will test and discipline him in the slashing days of his youth; that it will thrill and defy him in the days of his mastery; and that it will still afford him real pleasure to the last green on the last day. This is much, but we are thinking of the ideal golf course.

THE IDEAL GOLF COURSE by Robert Hunter, from *The American Golfer*, January 1927

It must certainly be a course which the champions will respect and this cannot be unless it is to call forth their finest effort. It must be a real test of their skill and if there be a weakness in their repertoire of strokes it shall uncover their shortcomings. On the other hand it must give enjoyment to those of lesser skill and of minor talent; and above all it must awaken interest in the youth and lead him to develop the best that is in him. It will indeed reward power; but only when that power is controlled and precisely used.

The ideal course shall be all this and yet more. It will regard those of limited strength and those whose vigor is passing. For these latter, it will always hold out the joyous opportunity to play those more cultivated strokes which years of training on the green have refined and which do not depend upon mere power.

My ideal course shall be on comparatively flat sandy soil amongst little hillocks and hollows and preferably by the sea. It shall lie at the border of my garden or, if it must be, down a very short lane.

The one so much desired shall be clothed in a fine velvety turf and that of the greens shall hardly be distinguished from that of the tees and fairways. Indeed it shall be difficult to define where the greens begin and the fairways end. Tees and greens shall be very like the country all about except that near the hole we shall find many subtle hollows and slopes besprinkled here and there with sandy depressions. There shall be no obvious erections or ridges, no embankments and terraces, but the ground shall be sculptured in gentle, flowing lines as if the wind had played upon it and tumbled it about before the turf had bound it down.

Throughout the fairways, there shall be other hazards but these shall be scattered about devoid of apparent plan; some of them lying where good shots are likely to go. One or two shall indeed lie just where one would most like to place his teeshots. This will mean that from the tee and from the lie, one shall be required to play with skill and circumspection. If one cannot carry the hazard, one must play to the right or the left.

There shall be all manner of good holes on my course and no two of them shall be alike. There shall be greens of many varieties; some quite large, others very small. They shall have mild hummocks and hollows and other delightful undulations upon and about them; because when I grow very old, I shall still wish to toddle down the lane and have my hour of delight. To some of the little harbors where the flag flies there shall be narrow and hazardous channels and here all manner of fine, precise

Thomas Hodge, *Mr. Bennet*, 1885. This portrait of a Royal and Ancient member in red jacket and brown hat is probably of Andrew Bennet, author of *The Book of St. Andrews Links*, 1898.

Walton Heath Golf Club, lithograph by Cecil Alden, 1920.

11th Green, East Course, Merion Golf Club, Ardmore, Pa. from a painting by Roy F. Spreeler, the hole on which Bobby Jones completed his grand slam in 1930.

shots shall be called for. Some will have to be played low, some quite high and some must run for a long way, while others must stop short.

Few would be bold enough to sketch too precisely an ideal course of the type I have briefly outlined and it would be rash to start a controversy upon such lines among the habitues of any club. The mere though of such a discussion is a bit terrifying and I can almost hear the derisive laughter and the "Impossible!", "ridiculous!", "silly dreamer!", and other such comments. But what I may hesitate to discuss face to face, because I should never be heard to the finish, I shall write. The thing has been done. I know at least one such course by Donald Ross, one by Walter Travis, and several by Dr. Mackenzie: but as you, doubting reader, may not know these courses, I shall not bring them into the argument. But I shall mention one, and this will, I think, be conclusive. The greatest course in the world is almost all that I have here described! The Old Course at St. Andrews is the one I have in mind, and if it lacks in any point, it is not an essential one.

Where else in the world do we find a course to which all great players journey and where all ages and all abilities meet and *all* praise with equal fervor? What other course can we all name which defies the champions and yet delights tottering old age? What other course can be played with a putter – the Swilcan being in that case the only serious obstacle – and at the same time be spoken of, by those qualified to speak, as the best course in the world? To my mind, and to that of far more

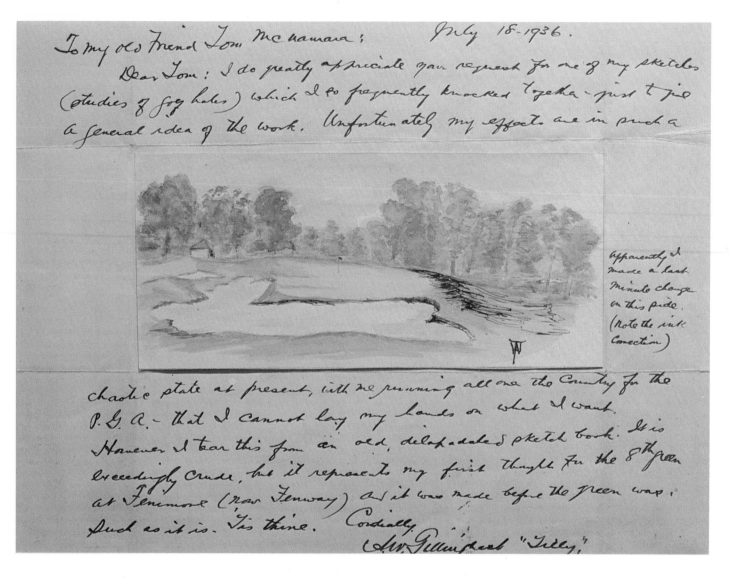

To my old Friend Tom McNamara: July 18-1936.

Dear Tom: I do greatly appreciate your request for one of my sketches (studies of golf holes) which I so frequently knocked together—just to give a general idea of the work. Unfortunately my efforts are in such a

Apparently I made a last minute change on this side. (Note the ink correction)

chaotic state at present, with me running all over the Country for the P. G. A.—that I cannot lay my hands on what I want. However I tear this from an old, dilapidated sketch book. It is exceedingly crude, but it represents my first thought for the 8th green at Fenimore (now Fenway) as it was made before the green was. Such as it is. 'Tis thine. Cordially, A.W. Tillinghast "Tilly,"

Watercolour painting by A. W. Tillinghurst of the Ferway Country Club Green, 18 July 1936 and original letter to Tom McNamara, donated by Joe Murdoch, co-founder of the Golf Collectors Society of America to the USGA Museum.

competent judges, St. Andrews is so near to the ideal that one would be most ungrateful to seek further for anything more perfect in this most imperfect world.

While early courses varied a great deal in size, as equipment improved and new balls and steel-shafted clubs were introduced, the usual length of a course increased to 7,500 yards. Since the days when golf was confined almost exclusively to the British Isles and the United States, there has also been an increase in the number of different countries where the game is played, which can now be found in every continent of the globe.

IT'S A ROYAL GAME IN JAPAN
by Earl Chapin May, from *The American Golfer*, January 1932

Behind a broad moat and a high stone wall, in the center of Tokyo, Japan, lives His Imperial Highness Hirohito, ruler over seventy million Japanese to whom he is a god, a priest and an Emperor. He arises each morning at six o'clock, is busy on affairs of state until late in the afternoon and is seldom seen outside the Imperial grounds. But each day of his life he plays golf on a private course inside the wall which sets him apart from other men.

As goes the Emperor, so goes Japan. He endorses the royal and ancient game by playing it, hence all Japan is strong for golf. Few in addition to the royal family have seen His Imperial Highness follow through, but every one knows that, in addition to horseback riding, tennis and biology, he likes the game brought to Japan by Englishmen nearly thirty years ago. His liking for golf is reflected in his minions from princes to counts, captains of industries and coolies.

When Walter Hagen and Joe Kirkwood won a close match play from Miyamato, open golf champion, and Yasuda, a runner-up in a previous Japanese tournament, on the Tokyo Golf Club's links, more than a thousand Japanese fans followed them around the eighteen-hold course. In that excited and fast moving throng of fans were their Imperial Highnesses, Prince and Princess Asaka, Prince Takeda and Prince Kuni. It was a gathering of Japanese notables who mingled with the two hundred "foreigners" representing American and England and other distant countries.

The course on which the champions played was nearly six miles from the center of Japan's capital. Except for the clumps of red Japanese pine and bamboo which adjoin the fairways and the greens and except for the Japanese players and caddies, the latter in *red* caps and kimonos if they are chasing golf balls for royalty, a visitor might think himself in England. Such is the charm of the rolling landscape.

Poster for Eastern Bengal Railway, Shillong the Gleneagles of India, *c.* 1930s.

DR ALISTER MACKENZIE

Mackenzie is best known for his design of the Augusta National, a demanding course which requires the player to plan each shot carefully. He was born in 1870 and became a doctor after graduating from Cambridge. In 1907 he met Harry Colt, a golf architect of some experience, and the two men formed a partnership. Together they designed the Alwoodley course at Leeds. After the First World War Mackenzie laid out Royal Melbourne in Australia. Then, in 1926 he went to America, where he designed the Cypress Point course in California. It was after this that Bobby Jones asked him to collaborate with him on the Augusta National course. Built at a cost of $100,000 the Augusta National has one of the most beautiful settings in the world, with all the holes named after the flowers that bloom there.

In 1920 Mackenzie wrote a book called *Golf Architecture*, which was based on two lectures he gave to the Golf Greenkeepers' Association. He also contributed to *Some Essays on Golf-Course Architecture*, published in 1919, which contained articles by C. H. Alison, Horace G. Hutchinson and John L. Low as well.

During his career, Mackenzie was involved in laying out or remodelling courses all over the world, in California, Ireland, Uruguay and the British Isles. He died in 1934 in Santa Cruz, California, in very poor circumstances. He was not a good financial manager and enjoyed the good life, travelling extensively.

HARRY COLT

Born in 1869, Harry Colt studied law at Cambridge, where he was captain of the golf team. He was called to the bar and worked for a few years in his chosen profession, but the lure of golf was too great. A member of the Royal and Ancient Golf Club, he won the Jubilee Vase there in 1891 and 1893 on the old course. In 1894 he helped to design the new Rye Golf Club course

27

and was the first secretary there until 1913. He never became a professional golfer, though he represented England in 1908 and reached the semi-final of the Amateur Championship in 1906.

HISTORICAL
BRITISH AND
AMERICAN
COURSES: ST.
ANDREWS by
George W.
Greenwood, from
Golf Illustrated,
January 1930

Of all the world's championship courses St. Andrews by reason of tradition, character and "atmosphere" is the most famous. Bobby Jones came to St. Andrews and hated it; he returned and loved it. This is the way of St. Andrews. First impressions are not flattering; they can, in fact, be scandalously defamatory of the "holy of holies." But as sure as the sun rises in the East so certain is it that the man who departs as a heathen will return to worship at its shrine.

I have stood in the windows of the Grand Hotel looking straight down the 1st and 18th fairways and I have heard people exclaim, "Gee, this is a funny looking golf course; a vast stretch of turf with no bunkers." Perfectly true; there are no bunkers, nothing but a roadway to the sea cutting at right angles across the course; but there is a celebrated hazard, which the eye cannot detect, until you are upon it, at the foot of the first green. It is the notorious Swilcan burn, a tortuous little stream winding in and out like a serpent within 75 feet of the flag waving defiantly on the other side.

Arthur Weaver, signed print with the remarques of the First Tee and Tom Morris Green at St. Andrews Royal and Ancient.

If one were paid a dollar for every ball finding its way into the Swilcan in the course of a year he would be a rich man at the end; but how fabulously rich he

Arthur Weaver, *The 16th hole, Old Course, Royal and Ancient Golf Club*, oil, 1961.

would be if the same rate of payment were spread over the centuries during which man has played golf at St. Andrews crossing the Swilcan on his way to the sandhills and the glorious golfing country beyond irresistibly beckoning to him to exploit.

St. Andrews is a city given up wholly and entirely to golf; its shops, its streets, its inhabitants – men, women and children – are permeated with golf. The stream of wealth that pours into St. Andrews has no other source than golf; it is supplied by practically every country in the world whose nationals come to St. Andrews, in the same way Catholics flock to Rome. Golf was played at St. Andrews long before the year 1754 when the Royal and Ancient Club came into being.

In that year, the Silver Club was first played for, the "Gentlemen Golfers of Edinburgh" joining in the competition. The players met once a fortnight at eleven o'clock, played a round of the links, and afterwards dined together, each paying a shilling for his dinner – the absent as well as the present. Eighty-three years later, in 1837, King William the Fourth presented a gold medal for annual competition which is now the chief trophy of the Royal and Ancient Club. Roger Wethered holds the distinction of having won the Royal Medal in the lowest score, a 72 in 1923, the year he won the Amateur Championship. Kings, princes and royal dukes have been members and have held the office of captain of the R & A, an office which demands that the holder shall drive himself in to the accompaniment of the boom of cannon. The people of the Cathedral city spread themselves along the fairway and the person lucky enough to capture the ball driven by the new captain is presented with a

29

sovereign. There are no authoritative records of when golf was first played at St. Andrews, but golf was a popular game in Scotland when St. Andrews University was founded in 1413.

The Royal and Ancient Golf Club of St. Andrews is the ruling body in golf in Great Britain. The title was approved by King William IV in 1834. The present clubhouse was built in 1840 and extended in the early part of the present century.

In 1913 Colt had the honour of designing the Eden Course at St. Andrews, and the same year he went to assist George Crumb in laying out Pine Valley in New Jersey, which is still considered to be one of the very best courses in the world today. Colt always used a drawing board and regarded trees and shrubs as a vital part of the course. He was involved in the design and construction of well over a hundred courses before his death in 1951.

DONALD ROSS

Ross was born in Dornoch, Scotland, in 1872. As a young man he went to St. Andrews to learn his trade under David Forgan at the Old Tom Morris shop, before returning to Dornoch as the head professional and greenkeeper. In 1898 he emigrated to Boston, Massachusetts, where he met the Turfs, who persuaded him to go to Pinehurst in North Carolina. He then alternated his time between the two places until 1910, when he decided to concentrate on Pinehurst, where he laid out course no. 2. His fame spread and he designed over 600 courses. Ross was manager at Pinehurst until his death in 1948.

ROBERT TRENT JONES

Born in 1906, Trent Jones was just four years old when his family went to live in the United States. As a golf architect he has had a huge impact on modern-day courses, having worked on over four hundred in twenty different locations. All his courses are difficult. When he had redesigned Baltusrol for the 1954 United States Open, he was told that the course was now considered too testing. Trent Jones was prepared to make whatever alterations were necessary and even to pay for them himself. However, when playing the course with the USGA Committee, at the hard 194-yard fourth hole, he had a hole in one and, turning to his playing partners, said "As you can see, this hole is not too difficult!"

Trent Jones has two sons, Robert Junior and Rees, both of whom have joined him in his golf architecture practice.

JACK NICKLAUS

The greatest golfer of the modern age, Nicklaus has won twenty titles. He was born in 1940 and became interested in golf architecture in his early twenties. Having first worked with Peter Dye on a number of projects, in 1974 he formed his own practice with Bob Cupp and Jay Morrish. His assistants do the preparatory work and he then adds all the detail designed to make a course more attractive. When his original partners left to form their own company Nicklaus added new talent to his team, which now numbers

Opposite: Poster for "Seaboard Air Line Ry, the Line to the Links", with the "Golf Girl" by Earl Christy, c. 1905.

SEABOARD AIR LINE RY.
THE LINE TO THE LINKS
GOLF
AT
Pinehurst, N. C.
Southern Pines, N. C.
Camden, S. C.
Savannah, Ga.
Jacksonville, Fla.
Atlantic Beach, Fla.
Winter Park, Fla.
Tampa Bay, Fla.
Belleview, Fla.
GOLF
AT
St. Augustine, Fla.
Ormond, Fla.
Palm Beach, Fla.
Miami, Fla.
RETURNING
GOLF
AT
Pinehurst, N. C.
Old Point Comfort, Va.
Virginia Beach, Va.
F. Earl Christy
Through Tickets on Sale
by Coupon Ticket Agents of Connecting Lines
and Seaboard Offices at all Important Points

Postcards (From left to right): Royal
North Devon Golf Club, Westward Ho!,
c. 1910; St. Andrews, the Mecca of golf,
and Rusack's Marine Hotel, 1902; Golf
House and golf course, Troon, 1905.

one hundred and fifty people.

Jack Nicklaus is a perfectionist and courses with his signature on them do not come cheap. His Shoal Creek course was chosen for the PGA Championship soon after it opened. He also designed Muirfield Village, where in 1987 the European team won the Ryder Cup, and built the St Mellion course in Cornwall, which opened in 1987. Nicklaus feels very strongly about putting something back into the game and knows his courses will survive long after him.

DUTIES AND
RESPONSIBILITIES
OF A GREEN
CONVENER by G.
P. Bryce, from
*British Golf Union
Journal*, Vol II, no.
4, March 1931

Golfers as a rule accept good conditions on their courses without comment, but should a green languish they immediately arise from their lethargy and loudly proclaim against the powers that be.

It is admitted that the golfer is entitled to enjoy good greens and good general conditions in keeping with the season of the year and the situation of the course, be it seaside or inland. Weather conditions, however, control the results of the best laid schemes to such an extent that good greens or moderately good greens are in the lap of the gods. Now that the Board of Greenkeeping Research is our ally there is less excuse for bad greens, and it behoves Green Conveners to scrutinize their methods most carefully. The golfer of to-day looks for a higher standard of conditions on his course than he did even a few years ago and the reason for this is obvious. The game has become more popular and the number of Clubs has multiplied. Some of these have succeeded in achieving high standard courses from a greenkeeping point of view, and naturally, golfers who are member of adjacent Clubs whose courses are not up to these standards are clamouring to know the reason.

A most important duty which falls to the Convener concerns the drainage of the

Rusack's Marine Hotel.

St. Andrews N.B.
The Mecca of Golf.

Club House and Golf Course, Troon.

course, as without a sufficient drainage system greenkeeping is rendered both difficult and heartbreaking. It is better to have too many drains than too few. Greens in particular require special attention and the lack of drainage proves in many cases to be at the root of a failure to maintain the turf in anything like first-class condition. Further, the more drains the fewer worms.

How many Clubs know where their drains are situated even if they know of their existence?

Most Clubs possess plans of the Course and it is the duty of the Convener to ensure that every drain is truly plotted on a duplicate of the plan of his course.

A Convener should encourage his Greenkeeper by taking a keen interest in all the problems as they arise. After comparison of opinions a decision usually has the effect of inspiring a mutual confidence between Convener and Greenkeeper. Moreover such a constant personal touch enables a Convener to acquire some of the valuable local knowledge possessed by the Greenkeeper regarding the variety of soil conditions which prevail or where, for example, the best top-spit is to be found, or where sharp sand can be procured on the course.

Good-will and co-operation between Conveners and Greenkeepers work wonders on most courses; where little interest is shown in their efforts and no sympathy is extended in their difficulties, Greenkeepers quickly lose heart much to the detriment of the course.

Good Greenkeepers are constantly seeking better methods, are always deeply interested in any successful experiments in greenkeeping problems and are anxious to explore the particular mode by which the attainment of success has been rendered possible. In order to develop this excellent trait Conveners should encourage their Greenkeepers to indulge in experiments on their own courses. A small plot of ground somewhere in the rough is all that is necessary and from it much valuable information may be acquired.

A Convener should accept full responsibility for the maintenance of the course and should protect his Greenkeeper from criticism by Club members who should be tactfully asked to recognize the indiscretion of offering to the Greenkeeper gratuitous advice on the maintenance of the Golf Course. The Convener is anxious and willing to listen to destructive criticism provided that the members can also be constructive.

During a period of fifteen years as a Green Convener, many constructive suggestions reached the writer. Possibly the following appealed most to Club members.

"That posts be erected in the rough at suitable points to expedite the finding of balls."

The posts were erected within the week.

Dieppe Poster, Société de Golf de Paris trophy awards in 1903. La Plage la plus proche de Paris Route Autodrome. By Genes, reprinted 1984 in the USGA Museum.

Postcard. Louis Wain, three cats as golfers, 1906.

GOLF BALLS

Originally a stone or a wooden ball and stick were used to play golf, but as early as 1743 Thomas Mathison in his poem "The Goff" described making a ball from feathers. A leather casing consisting of two, three or four sections was hand-sewn together and reversed, leaving a small hole through which the feather filling could be inserted. The feathers were usually goose, or sometimes chicken. They were boiled to make them soft and manageable and callipers were used to help stuff the leather casings. This was such a long, slow process that one craftsman could produce only four in a day, making them expensive. Some selected featheries, as they were called, were stamped with the maker's name. A few of these have survived and are very much sought after by collectors.

Two feathery golf balls. (Above) made by William Gourlay, *c.* 1830–40. (Below) a modern reproduction worth a fraction of the original.

A little ball so black!
I've dealt you many a whack
  On every side.
All the cuts and gashes,
Not to mention scratches,
  No paint can hide.
You looked so glossy white
I hailed you with delight.
  Quite hard and round

Were you when first I struck
You in my run of luck
  From the teeing-ground.
Though now you've lost your beauty,
Yet still you've done your duty,
  And on the Down
The record we did beat.
T'was fine to see retreat
  Both Smith and Brown.

TO A GOLF BALL
by "Shamrock",
from *Golf,* 20
November 1896

Black Diamond box label; ball box for 6 balls; ball box for 3 balls; two Black Diamond balls.

Early makers' names include Allan Robertson, Gourlay, Willie Dunn, Tom Morris and Thomas Stewart.

Many people continued to experiment with the production of balls, and in 1848 the gutta percha ball came into being. A rubbery substance, gutta percha is made from the latex of tropical trees. This new type of ball could be mass-produced, with a corresponding reduction in cost. As the gutta percha ball was harder and more durable and put a strain on the slender club-heads of the time, the heads were modified into shorter, squatter shapes. By the end of the 1850s featheries had become obsolete.

The early "gutty" balls, as they were called, were hand-crafted by heating the gutta percha in hot water, moulding it into the shape of a ball and then dropping it into cold water to harden it. Unmarked on the surface, these were known as smooth gutties. New balls were erratic in flight, but as they became scuffed and nicked from use their flight improved. Attempts were therefore made to add marks artificially in the manufacturing process. Robert Forgan made the first hand-hammered balls to a regular shape and pattern, but it gradually emerged that cover markings made a difference to the flight of the ball and that most golf balls were better if they had been left to dry out or "seasoned".

By the end of the nineteenth century, gutty balls were being made in iron moulds with a mesh pattern and cork was used inside the balls to help increase their potential distance. Gutta balls varied in mass between 26 and

29 pennyweights. Some of those makers who named their balls include Willie Dunn, Robert Forgan, James Gourlay and Allan Robertson.

It is more than likely that golf is on the eve of such a revolution as it has never before known. The investigations of Sir Ralph Payne-Gallwey, the second portion of which were published in the *Times* last week, point to a development of the science of the game, particularly as regards clubs and balls, on wholly novel lines.

There is one possibility opened up by his remarks which does not seem as yet to have occurred to anyone, and which is yet exceedingly simple. It is that an advantage may be gained by playing a different ball for different circumstances. No doubt there always have been players who realized this principle to a certain extent. I myself, who like a soft ball, prefer to drive a hard one in playing against a breeze. And I know several players who like to use a gutty in the teeth of the wind. The obvious disadvantage of this course is that variation of the balls is almost certain to have a bad effect upon the player's putting.

At the same time it is rather remarkable that the golfer, whose ingenuity in devising clubs to suit all sorts and conditions of stroke has carried him to such extraordinary lengths, should have made no attempt to do the same with the ball. I venture to prophecy that, within a year or two, it will be the common thing for every golfer to play a ball with one kind of marking down the wind, and a ball with another kind of marking into the wind.

For, consider a moment the data afforded us by Sir Ralph Payne-Gallwey's experiments. Firstly, a smooth ball will not fly – some marking is a necessity in all circumstances in order that the ball may carry properly at all. But a very slight marking indeed is sufficient to fulfil this requirement.

Secondly, a deeply-marked ball has always a tendency to soar. This, of course, is a deadly disadvantage against a wind, because a high ball in the teeth of the gale never

THE DORMY PAPERS by Holm Greene, from *Golfing*, 1 April 1909

Meteor ball by Goodrich, patented 1899.

A1 black golf ball box, Gutta Percha Co., London, dated 1899.

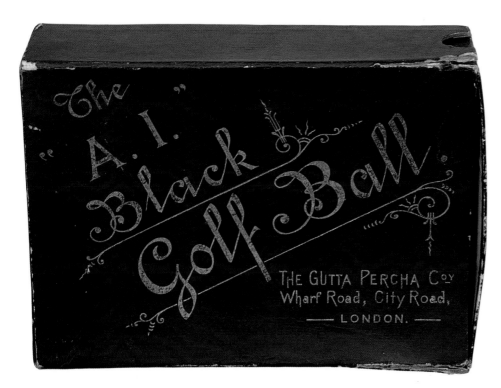

carries far; indeed cases have been known in which such a ball has been blown back over the head of the player. But, in driving with the wind behind, it is a real gain that the ball has a tendency to soar, because the wind behind is apt to kill a low ball by not giving it a chance to rise, whereas the soaring ball is being carried along by the wind as long as the ball keeps up.

Here, then, we have our first suggestion. The ball which the player intends to use against the wind should have markings as slight as is consistent with flying properly at all, whereas the ball which he will use in driving "down the wind" should be marked much more deeply.

One of two principles, quite independent of Sir Ralph's researches, have to be taken into consideration. For instance, the more pronounced the brambling on the hide of the ball the greater is the friction with the air, and the greater the resistance to the whole motion of the ball. It follows that even in playing with the wind it becomes a disadvantage to increase the roughness of the ball's surface beyond a certain maximum.

On the other hand, a certain amount of roughness has the advantage of enabling the club and ball to remain in contact with one another longer than they would otherwise do; because the brambling helps the ball to yield somewhat to the stroke. And the longer the club and ball are in contact the greater, other things being equal, is the force of the blow. The cover does not need to be very rough, however, before this advantage is more than counterbalanced by the disadvantages.

Moreover, if Sir Ralph Payne-Gallwey's suggestion, that the club should be faced with rubber rather than the ball be rubber-cored, be supplemented by the idea of having the brambling on the face of the club instead of on the cover of the ball, this last argument for the "rough" cover entirely disappears.

I would suggest, therefore, that the markings which now obtain are probably too pronounced for obtaining the best results even with the wind. And in this connection it is interesting to observe how well, often, a much used rubber-core flies – probably because the battering it has received has to some extent reduced the depth of the markings.

Left: "Vardon Flyer" golf balls, Silvertown, London. Mesh balls manufactured exclusively for A. G. Spalding in 1906.

Middle: The Burnet Golf Ball Box of three.

Right: The Kite Golf Ball Tin Box.

Postcards (From top to bottom): Dunlop "Fore" ball, 1906; "The Hawks are Flying", 1908; Silvertown No. 9 Golf Ball advertisement, showing new ball and one that has played 517 holes, 1909.

Eureka golf ball box, made by the Gutta Percha Co., London, *c.* 1898.

The Silvertown Company began making gutties under their own label in about 1888. It is obviously more desirable to collect named balls in as good condition as possible. Later ones were wrapped and boxed. The boxes are very ephemeral, but many had excellent artwork on them. They are collected in their own right today.

A few of the names to look for are: "Eclipse", made by Come and Co. in around 1877; "Forgan", around 1900; "A1", made by Gutta Percha Co. in 1894; "Ocobo", made by Halley in 1894; "Musselburgh", made by Henley's Telegraph Works Ltd. in 1896; "Vardon Flyer" by Spalding, 1899: and "Wright and Ditson", 1900. This is only a very short list, however. Over the years there have been over 3,000 makers of balls.

Around the turn of the century the arrival of the rubber-core ball in 1899 marked a revolution in ball-making and the beginning of the kind of rubber ball we know today. The manufacturing process involved winding thread or tape into a small ball and then covering it with gutta percha. The new ball was named after its inventor, Coburn Haskell, who worked with the

Selection of golf ball boxes. Cheerio box for rubber-core balls, *c.* 1928; North British twin-dot, *c.* 1920; Penfold box, *c.* 1938; Spaldings Top Flite, for dimple balls, *c.* 1950 and for mesh balls 1940. All others are post-war. Note Dunlop 65 tin.

Above: W. and D. Bullet mesh, Wright and Didson, a box for twelve balls and one for six balls and ball.

Left: Perfect Colonel golf ball box, *c.* 1905.

Below: Tommy Armour Golf Balls, made by Worthington Ball. Co., Elyna, Ohio, *c.* 1932. The US Open in 1927, the PGA Open in 1930, the British Open in 1931 and the Canadian Open in 1927 and 1930 are all said to have been won using these balls.

Goodrich Company of Akron, Ohio, in 1899. Decorated with a mesh pattern, these balls were very frisky, and became known as "Bounding Billies". They could travel further than other models, even when incorrectly struck by the club. It was soon discovered, by accident, that a bramble pattern on the outside of the ball led to an even better performance and thus a new looking ball came onto the market.

HOW HASKELL
GOT THE HUNCH
by H. M. Regner,
from *The American
Golfer*, December
1926

No other step in the development of golf running back over a period of some five hundred years has had so far reaching an effect as the introduction of the rubber-cored ball. There are some who go so far as to say that but for this invention, golf would never have reached the wide popularity that it now enjoys. This is a fit subject for debate, but there can be little doubt that the lively resilient rubber ball, making for longer distance, gave a notable impetus to the growth of interest in the game.

On a hot summer's afternoon back in 1898, about the time that the echoes from the charge at San Juan Hill and El Caney were dying away into the distance, Mr. Coburn Haskell, a retired business man, strolled into the office of a friend, Mr. Bertram G. Work, at that time superintendent for the B. F. Goodrich Tire and Rubber Company and in due course began to unburden his mind of the woes incidental to a fit of shanking his mashie shots, which was gripping him at the time.

"Well, if you ask me," answered Mr. Work, as his visitor reached a temporary pause in his sad recital, "I think it all probably serves you right, wasting so much time on the silly business of knocking a little ball around the fields. Why don't you turn your hand to something worth while; get out and make two blades of grass grow, where formerly but one grew, for instance?"

"Not interested in grass, except that which grows on fairways and putting greens, and there are lots better green keepers than I am. Anyhow, there's more to golf than

Selection of gutta percha and rubber-core balls. The Spalding 50 in the original box is rubber-core, *c.* 1920.

Opposite: Golf balls. Top: Paragon 27½, Eureka 27½, Silvertowns; row 2: White Colonel, the Claro, Chemical Bob; row 3: Spalding Midget, Spalding Dimple, unknown mesh ball; row 4: Spalding 50, Aristocratic, Eagle Reach.

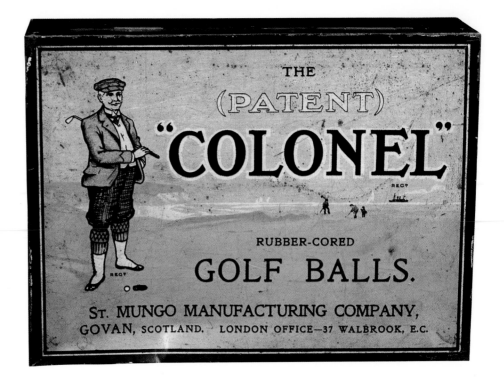

Colonel golf ball tin for rubber-core balls, made by St. Mungo Manufacturing Co., Govan, Scotland, *c.* 1915.

Advertisement for Colonel Golf Ball, 1910, showing various floater and non-floater balls made by the St. Mungo Manufacturing Co. Ltd. of America.

you may think. It's a great game."

"All right then, go ahead and do something to make it an even better game. Invent a new ball or design a new stick or something of the kind."

Now here *was* an idea. For a minute or so Haskell sat silent, and then –

"If a good rubber ball could be developed – a solid one – why I believe it would mean a big improvement in the game."

"Solid rubber won't do," interrupted his companion, "too soft; it would take too much compression in the hitting."

"Then how about compressing the rubber in the manufacture?"

"No, that won't do either."

Again Haskell paused in silence for a minute or more, then, "Well, what of this idea – suppose you cut the rubber in strips and stretched these and wound them into a ball; you could then get the ball as hard or soft as you can chose, couldn't you?"

"Now, you have said something," answered Mr. Work. He sent out and had a supply of rubber yarn brought in and invited Mr. Haskell to go to work on the first rubber golf ball ever attempted.

"It was an amusing sight," explains Mr. Work now as he recalls those experiences. "The day was hot and before Haskell really got started on his task he was perspiring from every pore. You who have never tried the experiment can't fully appreciate the difficulty of trying to wind this ball of rubber yarn, keeping the strand pretty well stretched while it is being wound. I don't know how many times it happened that Haskell got the thing going and brought it up to about the size of a marble only to have it slip from his grasp and quite unroll itself on the floor. Haskell would do a little "cussing" and start all over again.

"Finally in the dusk of the evening, with a beam of triumph, he presented to me a ball about the size of a walnut, fairly round and with the strands quite tense. It felt firm and solid, but of course the need for a covering of some kind was obvious.

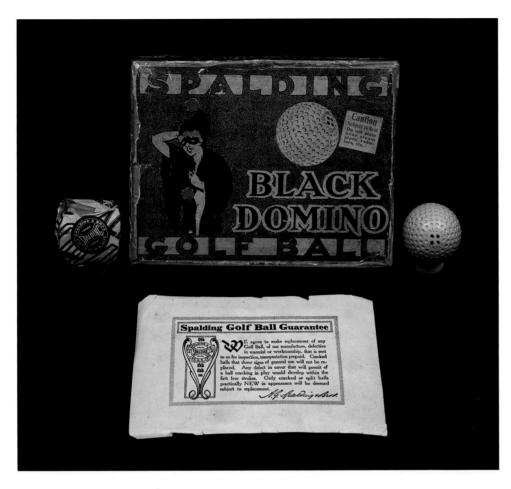

Black Domino rubber-core golf balls
made for the Spalding Co., 1908, with
original box and guarantee slip.

Otherwise the first slight cut would start the thing ravelling and in less time than it
takes to tell it, there would be no ball left."

The story of the development of a satisfactory covering is many parts of an epic of
itself, and the early experimenting on this end of the job fell to Mr. Work. He began
casting around for a practical idea as to the correct substance to form the cover and
eventually chose gutta percha. At the present time coverings are made of balata. Also
Mr. Work evolved a plan for heating a slab of gutta percha, molding it into shape
and pressing it onto the ball.

This operation is considerably simpler in the telling than it was in the doing, but it
was eventually completed. The ball was then painted, and Mr. Haskell hied himself
to his golf club with it. He summoned Joe Mitchell, the club professional, went to
the first tee, teed it up and asked Joe to hit it. The mold in which the cover had been
pressed on was the same as that used for making "gutty" balls, and the new ball
looked quite the same as the others.

Mitchell, little suspecting the part he was playing in the history of the mechanics
of the game, took his stance and swung. At a considerable distance out from the tee a
cross bunker extended the full width of the fairway. It was placed there to catch a
topped second, and only the most prodigious drive with the old "gutty" would cause
the ball to reach it even on the roll. The idea that one could actually hit a ball over it
on the carry was more than preposterous. But right over the middle of this bunker
sped the ball on Mitchell's drive. It landed on the fairway yards beyond the further
limit of the bunker.

Opposite: Wrapped golf balls. Top: Spring Vale Hawk, Hutchinson Maine and Co., rubber-core floater, 1907, Scottish Par Player, Dunlop lattice ball; row 2: Dunlop Warwick, Colonel, Dunlop Blue Flash mesh; row 3: Spalding needled Top flight dimple, US Rubber fairway, Price's Everlasting, Glasgow; row 4: Uniroyal Plus 6, Bridgetown Eagle Lge., Slazenger Plus 1.62.

Right: Spalding 50 golf ball, with original wrapping and box, 1919.

Below: Spalding Kro-Flite red dot golf ball and its original box, 1906.

Mitchell watched the flight and fall of the ball with open-mouthed wonder. When he saw it strike the turf well beyond the bunker, he began a kind of dance and set up a yell of surprise. Had he actually carried the bunker or was he seeing things? If he had carried the bunker, then what in the world was in that ball to make it travel so far? Then Mr. Haskell let him in on the secret of what made that mighty drive possible.

That's the way it started – this rubber-cored ball, which really revolutionized the game of golf. Mr. Haskell and Mr. Work, who incidentally has climbed to the position of president of his company, were the co-inventors, and it was decided to call it the Haskell ball. There still remain several chapters of the long story of development from that day on down to the present, in the course of which many improvements and refinements have been made from time to time. Four years later, that is in 1902, Sandy Herd won the British Open Championship, thus becoming the first player ever to win a big national title while playing the rubber-cored ball. Since then, few, if any titles in golf have been won with anything else.

Haskell formed a company called the Haskell Golf Ball Company and sold the balls under license. One of the first companies in Britain to do so was Spaldings. After Sandy Herd won the 1902 British Open Championship using the then new Haskell ball, its popularity increased. As with all new inventions, however, it took time to win full acceptance. As late as 1914, J.

Postcards. (From left to right): The 'Kite' clears all hazards; The 'Kite' where did it come from?; The 'Hawk' is the favourite.

H. Taylor, James Braid, Harry Vardon and George Duncan played a four-ball match pitting the gutty ball against the new rubber-core ball. The new ball proved supreme in terms of both durability and length, and the gutty ball fell into disuse.

Although improvements have continued to be made to the golf ball, very little has changed since the bramble and dimple pattern was added at the beginning of this century. At one point liquid was introduced into the centre of the ball, a form of design which remained in use until around the mid 1960s, when one-piece rubber balls were introduced.

Until the early 1920s there was no standard weight for golf balls. However, most were either 1.62 ounces in weight and 1.62 inches in diameter (the small ball, or British size), or 1.68 ounces in weight and 1.68 inches in diameter (the large ball, or American size). Eventually the Royal and Ancient Golf Club agreed that the larger ball should be mandatory as from the Open Championship of 1974.

OUR NEW GOLF
BALL by Al
Espinosa, from
Golfers Magazine,
March 1931

The new larger and lighter ball, 1:68, made official January 1st, 1931, has been much discussed and commented on since we first received the news of the change, and I feel like many of the other boys in that we could not give a fair opinion of it until after we had gotten under way in our winter tournament tour.

Now, after using it officially since the Pasadena Tournament in December and

Practo golf balls, indoor/outdoor, use driver or iron. Made by Reliable Knitting Works, Milwaukee, Wisconsin.

Advertisement for Dunlop "Blue" Maxfli golf ball, 1923.

getting this far down through the South, where we are finding diversified kinds of golf courses with different grasses for fairways and putting-greens, I know we can give a surer and truer opinion of it than any of us could at the start of our winter tour.

Put to the test, the ball is liked better all the time. It was somewhat of a "bug-a-boo" at the start. We were hoping we would like it, and now after playing with it and under all conditions over the different courses it has proven to give us a better and more exacting test of golf. It was just the case of making the change. I like it better and I know most of the professionals do also.

In the beginning we were somewhat confused because we wanted to use the same iron clubs for the same distance as we did with the old ball, and this made us all short with our iron shots. However, with use and practice we have found that skill and control came better and easier with this longer iron shot.

There are only a few disadvantages to the new ball compared to the advantages of it. The wind, of course, places the new ball at a decided disadvantage. Then, there is a loss of distance of some few yards on the drive, and on the putting-green, the final drop of the ball into the cup is more problematic. The rim of the cup, the raise of ground around the cup – stubby grass – retards the final drop more than with the old ball, where the weight was centralized. But sitting up nicely on the putting-green helps to offset this disadvantage.

The advantages are many. To start with – just the feel of the new ball on the club is great, especially the iron clubs. It sits up nicely on the fairway, and this holds good for lies in the rough as well, also if a player finds the ball lying in heavy grass or clover or a bad lie in the fairway, he can use a longer club for the shot. With the old ball, when we found such a condition, we had to use a more lofted club and hit it harder than the distance called for, forcing the shot. Thus accuracy and control were lost. The new ball sits up much better in the traps than the old one.

In playing the short irons a golfer is able to hit the short shots firmer and with more accuracy than with the fast ball – which would frequently overrun.

With the new ball there is a greater variety of shots with fewer clubs, which means the skilled golfer can use the half and three-quarter swing and will not need a different club and a full swing for every shot.

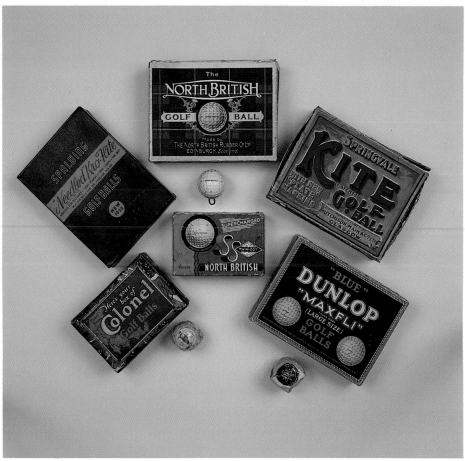

Selection of boxes and balls. Colonel Xmas box; Spalding needled Kro-Flite, 1935; North British ball, Edinburgh; North British twin tot; North British ball with steel hoop for Scottie dog advertisement; Springvale Kite ball by Hutchinson Main and Co., Glasgow; Blue Dunlop "Maxfli", large.

Of course, one of the most important advantages of the 1:68 is that it will cut down the expense of lengthening the yardage of courses to counteract the tremendous distances that were possible for the better players to secure with the old 1:62.

The principal disadvantage in the 1:68 is the fact that the ball is only legal in the United States. When our professionals and amateurs visit foreign countries, they will be required to go back to the old ball which naturally will cause confusion. Likewise, when the British Ryder Cup Team comes to Ohio in June to compete in the Ryder Cup Matches, Western Open and National Open, its members will need to use the 1:68. It will be interesting and enlightening to follow the scoring of our players in the British Open this Spring and also compare the scoring of the British Team with that of the American Team in the Ryder Cup Matches.

Anybody intending to collect golf balls is advised to buy those in the best possible condition with easily legible names. To have the boxes as well is always a bonus. Collectors may also be interested in "logo" balls. Over the last twenty years many companies have used them as promotional gifts and they have become very popular. For a relatively small outlay it is possible to assemble an impressive collection of these.

An excellent book by John Stuart Martin, called *The Curious History of the Golf Ball*, printed in 1968, will give an insight into the fascinating evolution of the golf ball. It was published in a trade and limited edition, however, the book will take some finding today.

A BAWL

WOMEN'S GOLF

Although Mary Stuart of Scotland was the first famous woman to play golf in the sixteenth century, it was not until hundreds of years later in 1893 that golf for women was fully established in the British Isles by the Ladies' Golf Union, or LGU. As a game that can be enjoyed by any player, whatever her level of skill, it soon spread in popularity and women champions appeared to rival the achievements of the men.

Since the days of Mary Stuart, who found golf so highly entertaining that her enemies alleged she showed shameless indifference by playing golf on the fields of Seton, while her husband lay murdered in the house at the Kirk O'Field, women have been interested in the game of golf. But the universal delight which women now generally manifest in golf is of a rather recent period and the interest of women in golf in large numbers is growing daily.

Apparently, the knowledge of, and the joy in, the game for women was lost for a time, until some adventuresome woman discovered the health-giving qualities of the game; then, the interest in it grew and grew, like the bean stalk in the childhood tale.

Doubtless in the days long gone, a golf widow sat thinking bitter thoughts of the way she was frequently deserted; sad and inexpressibly lonely; feeling intensely sorry for herself and impatiently wondering why all men were so frantically eager to spend every free moment on a golf course.

Royal Doulton Morrisian ware. Blue and
gold jug, 7 inches tall, *c.* 1910. The golfers
are in seventeenth-century costume.

The Lady and Caddy, American
lithograph, copyright 1913, by Sunfit and
Co.

The unhappy moments and hours lengthened into an eternity, until the time came
when the golf widow revolted, purchased a set of golf clubs, had a few lessons and
was thereby transformed into a real golf enthusiast.

There may even now be golf widows, but if so, they are busily engaged in
entertaining themselves at some alluring pastime, generally playing the ancient
game, in an up-to-date manner.

Everyone has progressed through the various discouraging stages of learning to
manipulate golf clubs with a degree of success, and now there are numberless
exceptional women golfers who have mastered these tricky bits of wood and iron.

Much concentration, study and practice are necessary in developing a good game
and one is always subtly conscious of the difficulty expressed in the ancient axiom
that golf is, "Putting a wee ba' in a sma' hole wi' instruments ill adapted to the
purpose."

Many women are averse to attempting golf because they have the mistaken idea it
is an intensely strenuous game, suitable only for the most athletic types. But it can be
played in any preferred manner, a few holes, or innumerable holes may be played as
the golfer desires, or her time, strength, or inclination permit.

Woman's emancipation has come in the growth of her body and mind and is
chiefly due to happy communion with the great out-doors.

A hand-painted Willerdy and Boch plate, Dresden, 7 inches diameter, made in Germany, 1905.

A hand-painted Nippon shot glass, 2 inches tall, *c.* 1920s, Japan.

A Moulin des Loups and Mamage plate, 7 inches diameter, *c.* 1915, France.

Magazine cover of *The Ledger Monthly*, 1899.

CECIL LEITCH by "The Bystander", from *Golfers Magazine*, July 1927

In the 1920s the leading American woman player was Glenna Collett, six times winner of the United States Amateur title. Having won her first tournament, the Shene Cossett Championship in 1920, when she was just 17, she went on to play for or captain the Curtis Cup side in 1932, 1936 and 1948. Joyce Wethered said of her, "Her charm to my mind as a golfer and a companion lies in a freedom of spirit which does not make her feel that success is everything in the world. Those who are so generous in defeat are the people most to be envied."

Joyce Wethered, an outstanding amateur, learned how to play golf from her brother Roger at the age of 17 whilst they were on holiday in Dornoch. Two years later in 1920 she entered the English Amateur Championship just to keep a friend company and much to everyone's surprise, she won, beating Cecil Leitch, heroine of British women's golf during the 1910s.

The story of Miss Leitch's golf career makes interesting reading. In company with her sisters, she began golf at a very early age, and while still in her teens, was regarded as a potential champion. But she experienced several years of disappointment before winning her first Open title in 1914. It was unfortunate that, just at the moment that she had reached the top of the tree, war should intervene, suspending competition for five years, but she retained her title in 1920, and '21. The latter year was important to Miss Leitch, for it marked the debut of Miss Wethered, who, as things turned out, was to supplant her as champion. The pair met for the first time in national competition in the finals of both the British and French Open Championships of 1921, Miss Leitch winning both titles. Since 1921, the two ladies have waged constant warfare, with Miss Wethered always the victor. It was immediately after the 1925 Championship that Miss Wethered announced her retiral, and the following year Miss Leitch demonstrated that she was still the best of the remaining ladies by winning her fourth Open Title. She did not compete in this year's Championship and it is to be hoped that she is not following her great rival into retirement.

Miss Leitch is mistress of two shots which baffle ninety per cent of lady golfers, and many men also, namely, the long brassie to the pin, and the long brassie or iron

Selection of silver spoons all depicting ladies. (Left to right): American sterling silver spoon, *c.* 1915; made by Robert Scout, 1914; made in Birmingham, 1914; made in Birmingham, 1926; made in Gnosburg Falls, Utah, *c.* 1915; made in Birmingham, 1930, with enamel; made in Birmingham, 1935.

shot into the teeth of a head wind. She is a long hitter with wood, and from any reasonable distance can be depended on to cover the pin, and lay the ball within holing distance. On a windy day her early training stands her in good stead. She learned to play at Silloth, which has the reputation of being one of the most wind-swept links in Britain – no mean distinction. The geographical situation of the course – it is on the Solway Firth, in the Northwest corner of England – is such that there are few days in the year when a breeze at the least is not blowing, and more often than not it is half a gale. It was while still a young girl, battling with the Silloth gales, that Miss Leitch was impressed with the necessity of hitting the ball low, and she moulded her style accordingly.

Between 1920 and 1924 Joyce Wethered won thirty-three matches, including the British Women's Championship in 1922, 1924, 1925 and 1929, and the English Women's Championship in 1920, 1921, 1922, 1923 and 1924. She also played in the Curtis Cup match in 1932.

Although she retired in 1926, Joyce Wethered decided to play at the British Championship in 1929 because it was being held at St. Andrews, and there she beat Glenna Collett in a very exciting match. By this time she had little left to achieve in the golfing world, but she continued to show an interest in the game, and played in the Worplesdon Mixed Foursome for many years, a title which she won eight times between 1922 and 1936. In 1935 she toured the United States of America giving exhibition matches, and both Henry Cotton and Bobby Jones considered her the best player ever, male or female.

After World War II many notable women players emerged with a smooth swing and a decisive hand action. It was then that Patty Berg, Babe Zaharias, Mickey Wright and Betsy Rawls came to the forefront. Babe Zaharias was born in Port Arthur, Texas, in 1914 and died after a battle against cancer in 1956. She was United States Amateur champion in 1946, British Amateur champion in 1947 and won the United States Open Women's Championship in 1948, 1950 and 1954. She had begun her sporting career as a field athlete and took part in the javelin, hurdles and high jump events at the 1932 Olympic Games. During 1946 and 1947 she won an unbroken series of seventeen matches.

Having undergone surgery for cancer in 1953 Babe Zaharias still came back to win her third United States Open the following year by a margin of twelve strokes. She won a further five matches in that year, and another in 1955, but sadly died in 1956 aged only 42.

In 1933 Babe set out to master the one competitive sport then open to women – golf. Her teaching pro, Stan Kertes, remembered how hard she worked. "Babe used to hit 1,000 or 1,500 balls every day. Her hands would blister up and bleed. She wore tape on them all the time. Babe would hit eight to ten hours a day."

In 1934 she entered her first tournament and qualified, but then lost out in match play. Her next try was at the Texas State Championship, something of a social affair. Although Babe was a national heroine, at the River Oaks Country Club in Houston she was the girl from the wrong side of the tracks; some members actually tried to prevent her from playing.

BABE ZAHARIAS: SHE WAS ONE OF A KIND by Gerald Astor, from *Reader's Digest*, 1982

Above: Postcard *c*.1912. Fashion Sunday Golf bag.

Opposite above: Postcard *c*.1910.

A Selection of six English and two American silver spoons.

Left: Mrs Walter Hagen and her friend Mrs A. W. Walker of Detroit viewing the progress of Walter Hagen, British Open Champion in the annual North and South Open Golf Championship Tournament at Pinehurst, North Carolina. 4 September 1925.

Middle: Miss Joyce Wethered (Worplesdon) winner and (right) Miss Sylvia Bailey (Combewood) leaving the first tee in the semi-final of the Surrey Ladies Country Golf Championship at Wentworth. 29 April 1932.

Right: Mrs Edith Guedella, British Amateur Champion and Miss D. R. Fowler, former British Open Champion, on the course at Hunstanton, England. 1932.

Hand-painted glass vase showing lady golfer, 10½ inches high, *c.* 1905.

In the semi-finals Babe and her opponent were tied at the final hole. A spectacular twenty-foot putt across a rain-soaked green put Babe in the final match. Then she again demonstrated her ability to come up with a super shot. At the 34th hole the finalists were tired, and Babe's opponent had chipped neatly close to the cup for a sure birdie (one stroke under the par-five for that hole). Babe's ball, however, had overshot the green and lay half-submerged in a watery ditch. Using a sand wedge, Babe swung. Water and ball exploded from the rut; the ball unerringly made its way to the cup for an eagle three (two strokes less than par). The shot put Babe ahead. She gained another stroke on the 36th hole and won.

Her career as a golfer stalled temporarily, however, when she ran afoul of strict rules governing amateur status, so she set out on a series of golf exhibitions with top player Gene Sarazen.

During this period Babe's image slowly metamorphosed from that of a raucous, tough-talking, "one-of-the-boys" types into one more representative of the women of the era. Largely responsible for the change was her first and only romantic interest, a six-foot, 225-pound wrestler and promoter named George Zaharias. After they were married, Zaharias kept his wife even busier in promotions and exhibitions.

During World War II Babe played with celebrities like Bob Hope, Bing Crosby, and Mickey Rooney to sell war bonds. But her amateur status had been restored, so in 1945 Babe resolutely returned to the tournament tour. In 1946 and 1947 she set a record that no athlete, man or woman, has ever approached: she won seventeen consecutive events. The pearls on this matchless string include every major U.S. golf tournament, plus the most celebrated victory of all, the British Women's Amateur.

During the 1970s and 1980s the level of public interest in women's professional golf has grown considerably, and there has been a corresponding increase in the number of competitions played and the amount of prize money being competed for. Today's women champions come from all over the world.

CLUBS, BAGS AND OTHER EQUIPMENT

lubs. Although golf clubs have been made for hundreds of years, very few of those produced prior to 1820 have survived today in their original form. The early clubs were hand-made and were constantly being modified. Sets consisted of six or nine clubs and were carried by the player or caddie. Golf bags did not come into being until about 1865.

There are various opinions as to the club a beginner should make her first efforts with, and the majority are in favour of a cleek. This is rather curious, as a cleek is one of the most difficult clubs to play with and very few golfers use it regularly, numbers using instead a driving mashie or aluminium spoon. A cleek, however, if a favourite, is invaluable, and it is an excellent instrument with which to begin operations, as it can send a ball a long distance and yet is generally useful for other strokes. Another good plan is to commence with a short, stiff, wooden club, brassy for choice, but this club cannot be used with the same success for a variety of shots. As soon as any progress has been made, the number of clubs can be increased, and the following set will be found quite sufficient for all ordinary purposes – namely, driver, brassy or spoon, cleek, iron, mashie and putter. A niblick is not a necessity but can be added if wanted. Having purchased clubs and balls, the next thing to do is to try and find out how to use them to the best advantage.

HINTS ON GOLF
by Miss Mary
Hazlet, from *The Golfer's Handbook*,
1904

Cabinet of early golf clubs: top row: long spoon by Douglas McEwan, 1809–86; bunker iron; putter by Tom Morris Senior, 1821–1908; row 2: play club by Hugh Philp, 1872–56; middle spoon by Douglas McEwan; play club by Willie Dunn, 1821–78; wood by David Anderson Senior, 1821–1901; row 3: baffing spoon by Hugh Philp; left-handed play club by Peter McEwan, 1834–95; short spoon by Jamie Dunn, 1821–71; row 4: putter by Hugh Philp; play club by John Jackson, 1805–78; play club by Tom Morris Senior.

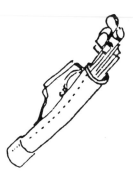

Lady's rut or track iron, made by H. Forgan and Sons, St. Andrews, for Harrods of London, with crown cleek mark, *c.* 1902.

The early designs had delightful names (not numbers as today), and included play clubs, grassed drivers, driving putters, spoons, baffing spoons, cleeks, wooden niblicks and wooden putters. Play clubs had hardly any loft and would be known as drivers today, although they were two inches longer than modern clubs. The long spoon, mid spoon, short spoon, baffing spoon and wooden niblick were shaped for different length shots. By 1850 the iron-headed track iron had also been introduced. Then, in 1885, the brassie was made. This had a brass base-plate to guard the head from damage. There were three types of putter: driving, approach and green. The cleek was a long-headed club for long-range shots. The lofter usually had a concave face and was almost like the modern five iron. The track iron was similar to today's sand wedge.

At first it is certainly a mistake to use too many clubs. A driver, for the tee shots and for good lies through the green; a brassie, for less good lies; a cleek or driving-iron, for shorter distances; a mashie or lofting-iron for quite short lofting shots up to the hole, and a putter, either of wood or iron, according to fancy, are fully sufficient. Even this number may quite well be reduced by using the cleek as a putter, and some use only one iron for driving and for lofting; but in this case the iron would need to be so lofted that it would not be a good club for putting, and probably four clubs are about the fewest that can be used with advantage. To begin with, it is best to use rather a short and stiff driver. Longer and more springy clubs may be adopted when fair certainty in driving has been attained, but at first they increase the difficulty of accurate striking. Let the club be neither too heavy nor too light – of medium weight, such as you feel you can swing freely and without effort. And, having such a club in your hand, the next point is the manner in which you are to address yourself to drive the ball with it. Do not be deluded into thinking that this is a matter of no importance. It is a great thing to get into a good style at the outset, for faults are much more difficult to cure later.

All the early iron clubs were hand-made, often by blacksmiths; but since the iron could damage featherie golf balls, few golfers used metal heads except for a difficult lie. One smith who made iron clubs was F. Carrick, and the few surviving clubs stamped with his name are valuable today. The early irons did not vary much in shape and were called track irons and lofting irons.

For a short while a one-piece club was made from a single branch that had grown in the right shape and could then be carefully worked by the club-maker. This design had no whipping. Although they are very much prized by collectors, clubs of this kind were never made in great quantity so there are few to be found today.

GOLF by Horace Hutchinson (Amateur Champion), from *Every Boy's Book of Sport and Pastime*, ed. Professor Hoffman, 1897

Different "faces" of the clubs.

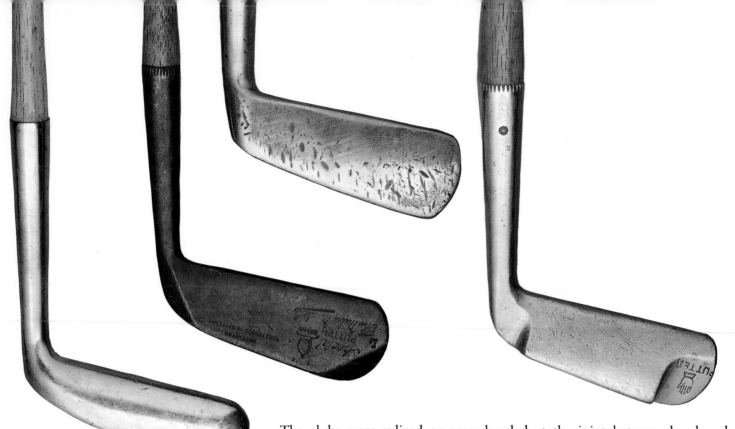

From right to left: Putter with open hand cleek mark, Nicoll, Leven, *c.* 1920s; brass putter, no name, *c.* 1905; mitre model putter, lady's, hand-forged, Scottish, *c.* 1900; smooth-faced putter.

The clubs were spliced or scare-headed at the joint between head and shaft. The shaft was glued into place and then bound with twine to ensure that it was secure. Usually ram's horn was placed on the base of the club-head to protect the wood from the elements. The heads had to be made from hard-wearing wood, and beech was usually used, although fruit woods such as apple and plum were also popular. By the 1890s, however, it had become clear through a process of trial and error that the best wood was persimmon from America.

In the early days shafts were made from ash, and then another American wood, the hickory, was introduced. Wooden shafts continued to be found until 1929 when they were largely replaced by the steel types that had come into use after about 1915, although many people still preferred the original hickories.

Early club-makers who stamped their names on their clubs included Willie Auchterlonie, Willie Dunn, Andrew Forgan, the McEwan family, Willie Park Senior and Hugh Philp.

What a halo and tribute surrounds these few words – a yellow-headed spoon – penned as they were by the late Mr. John L. Low (as fine a judge of a club as he was of the Rules) in his thoughtful volume, "Concerning Golf," when describing the clubs in the bag of that very great amateur player, Mr. Harold H. Hilton. Good as all the clubs were, only one did Mr. Low envy and covet – that "yellow-headed spoon, by Auchterlonie."

Beyond all shadow of doubt, as every old time golfer can truthfully testify, there was a very definite something about the yellow-headed wooden clubs made in the middle 1890s by D. & W. Auchterlonie, St. Andrews. There was no mistaking the "classic" lines of the heads, be the club driver, brassie or spoon; you knew the maker without needing to look! And as for the shafts, air-dried, straight-grained hickory was what the words specified. Greenheart and Lancewood shafts too, I remember, could also be had, for one sixpence extra!

Clubs of such high standard – hand tailored jobs they truly were in these old days – have never been surpassed and they stood up to the hardest possible play. One fault only did all of them seem to have, the power of making people envious. The writer's own treasured "woods" were cleverly purloined from his locker during a summer's absence on a visit to Canada. Perhaps the "borrowers" had also seen Mr. Low's reference to the "yellow-headed spoon by Auchterlonie," and fell victims to the envy it engendered. His loss was surely their gain, ill-gotten though it was.

When feathery and gutta percha balls were in use, the clubs were long-nosed, with thickish grips made from sheepskin or leather. Then, in the second half of the nineteenth century, as the balls improved so the clubs were modified. Heads became smaller and the "bulger" came into being. This was a rounded model, and not very attractive to look at. Club-makers then reshaped them to look more like those we are used to today. By the end of the nineteenth century the "socket head" had been introduced.

Many of the earlier club-makers had previously been involved in wood processing as furniture-makers or joiners. Several also made fishing rods. To begin with there were no greenkeepers as we know them now, but certain workers were known as "keepers of the green" and were called upon to do many jobs around the golf club, almost as handymen. In order to ensure a regular income many of these men had to be club- and ball-makers as well. By the turn of the century, however, as more golf societies and clubs were formed, these odd-job men began to play an increasingly important role.

Poster for D. and W. Auchterlonie's shop.

Selection of wood-shafted clubs, 1910–35. (From left to right): mashie niblick, T. J. Roach, Wellesby, hand-forged with lion cleek mark; mid iron, A. H. Scott, Earlsferry, Elie, *c.* 1914 (Scott took over from Andrew Forgan to become club-maker to the king in 1911); lady's mashie, W. Kneller, cleek mark of heart with an arrow across it of W. Hewitt, Carnoustie, *c.* 1910; lady's mashie niblick, A. Frazer, *c.* 1920s; mashie by J. A. Bray.

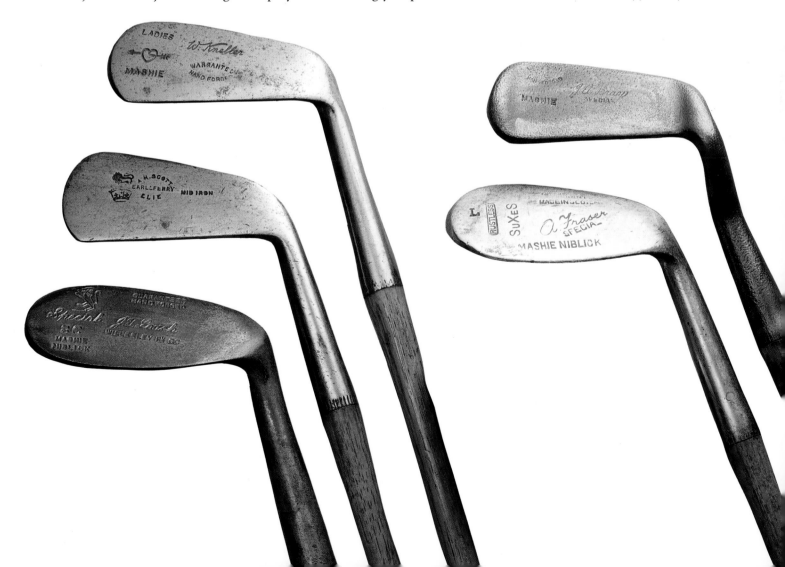

Walter Hagen concave face sand wedge.

Towards the end of the last century club-makers were beginning to use machines to help them. It may well be that Scott of Elie in Fifeshire made the socket-head club in this way. Walter Hagen certainly helped to popularize new methods when he won his first open in 1914 using a scared-head club. Centre-shafted clubs such as the Travis brass-faced putter were outlawed for many years in the USA after American Walter Travis won the British Amateur in 1904 using a similar putter. The ban was lifted in 1933. Inevitably, as the shapes, sizes and weights of clubs have changed over the decades, so too have the methods being advised for their use. Different materials have given rise to different techniques.

When dating various kinds of club it is possible to divide them into periods. Before 1890 there were long-nose wooden clubs, with a few iron heads; from 1890 to 1915 scared and socket heads, one-piece clubs and aluminium heads. Then between 1890 and 1920 far more iron clubs were developed, mostly machine-made. Earlier designs were smooth with no makers' names on them. Finally, after 1930, clubs became very much like those we know today, although some still had wooden shafts. The "classic clubs" date from the post-1945 era.

SCIENCE AND
THE CLUBMAKER
from *Golfing*,
February 1934

Golf, which used to be an art, has become a science, and if this is true of the playing of the game it applies even more strongly to the making of the weapons of golfing war.

There is a temptation nowadays to lament the passing of the clubmaker's craft and to visualize the making of the steel shaft as a very mechanical business. But this conception fails to recognize the inventive genius displayed in the construction of such a machine as that which in one slow revolution and eighteen successive processes puts the steps in the True Temper shafts and ignores the technical skill that

Selection of putters showing different faces. (From right to left): J. and D. Clark, *c.* 1880; L. Auchterlonie; Standard Golf Company; Wright and Didson, hammer-forged; Wilson/Gene Sarazen; Charles Klees; undetermined maker; Ampca.

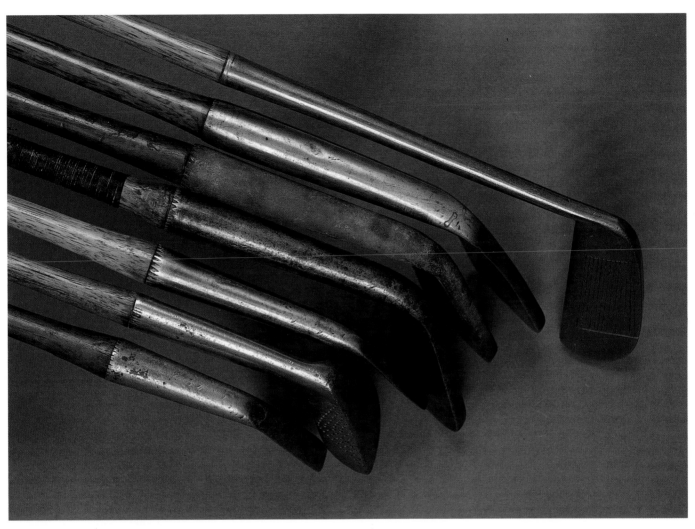

is called for in the hundred odd other different operations that go to the creation of the finished article, after the preliminary process by which tubes of roughly 1½ inches in diameter with walls over ⅛ of an inch thick are pulled out to the required diameter by being drawn *cold* through the eyes of specially prepared steel blocks, the eye in each case being smaller in diameter than the tube that is passed into it.

Some time ago an American visitor to the Accles & Pollock tube mill, presented the firm with a small sample of tubing which he explained was a hypodermic needle tube, adding that it was "the smallest tube in the world." After the visitor had left, Messrs. Accles & Pollock made some experiments and produced a cold drawn weldless steel tube of an outside diameter of one-fiftieth of an inch and an inside diameter of less than one-hundredth of an inch. A few weeks later they wrote to their American friend to the effect that they were returning "the smallest tube in the world" with the Accles & Pollock tube inside it! The firm are, of course, the specialists in the manufacture not only of steel shafts for golf clubs, but of steel tubes of all diameters up to four or five inches, and of everything that can be made of such tubes from hypodermic needles to steel tubular furniture and aeroplane frame-work.

In the hardening and tempering furnaces separate chambers are provided for each shaft, to keep them as straight as possible, but the final straightening process is done by skilled workmen by hand, the human eye in this respect being a more accurate test than any machine test could be.

Lengths and thicknesses of hosels. (From left to right): Triumph; Wrightson and Didson; Spalding; J. and D. Clark Lofter; D. and W. Anderson, St. Andrews; early bunker iron, c.1865; Wilson/Gene Sarazen putter.

Tom Morris putter, St. Andrews. Note the metal insert.

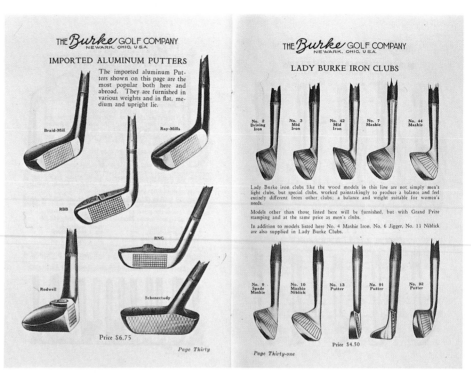

Burke Golf Co. Catalogue showing
putters and ladies iron clubs.

Prior to the finishing operations of cromium plating, rust-proofing, lacquering
and so forth, the shafts are submitted to a most rigorous series of examinations.
There is a deflection test which varies with the degree of "whip" required, but has a
minimum deflection of 3½ inches – considerably more than can possibly take place
in the actual striking of the ball. The hozel end of the shaft is subjected to a proof
loading test equivalent to a tensile strength of almost a hundred tons per square inch.
And finally there is the "slap" test, each shaft being struck on a hardwood block and
then dropped on a steel table, the "ring" of the shaft as it rebounds from the steel
enabling the operative to detect by ear the presence of any flaw.

Technical developments continue. On 6 February 1971, Apollo 14
Commander Alan B. Shephard Junior brought golf into the space age when
he swung a specially constructed iron at a ball on the surface of the moon.
His club consisted of a standard 6 iron head attached by means of a short
steel extension to a sectioned aluminium shaft with Teflon joints, creating an
overall weight of 16½ ounces.

WHAT ABOUT
YOUR CLUBS? by
Grantland Rice,
from *American
Golfer*, February
1927

"Some time ago," remarked George Duncan, "a certain golfer came to me
complaining about his game. He simply couldn't turn in a consistent round. I
watched him swing a few times and he had a good swing. Then I decided to look
over his collection of clubs. I found he was using a driver and a brassie with an
upright lie and a spoon with a flat lie. Few of his irons were matched. His driver and
his brassie were entirely too heavy and there was no feel of the head in either. He had
picked these clubs, one at a time, here and there, without any thought of their
matching one another or suiting his own game. There was quite enough in these
badly matched clubs to account for a world of inconsistent play."

Golf is a game in which only a minor mistake, a slight error in timing, may mean a

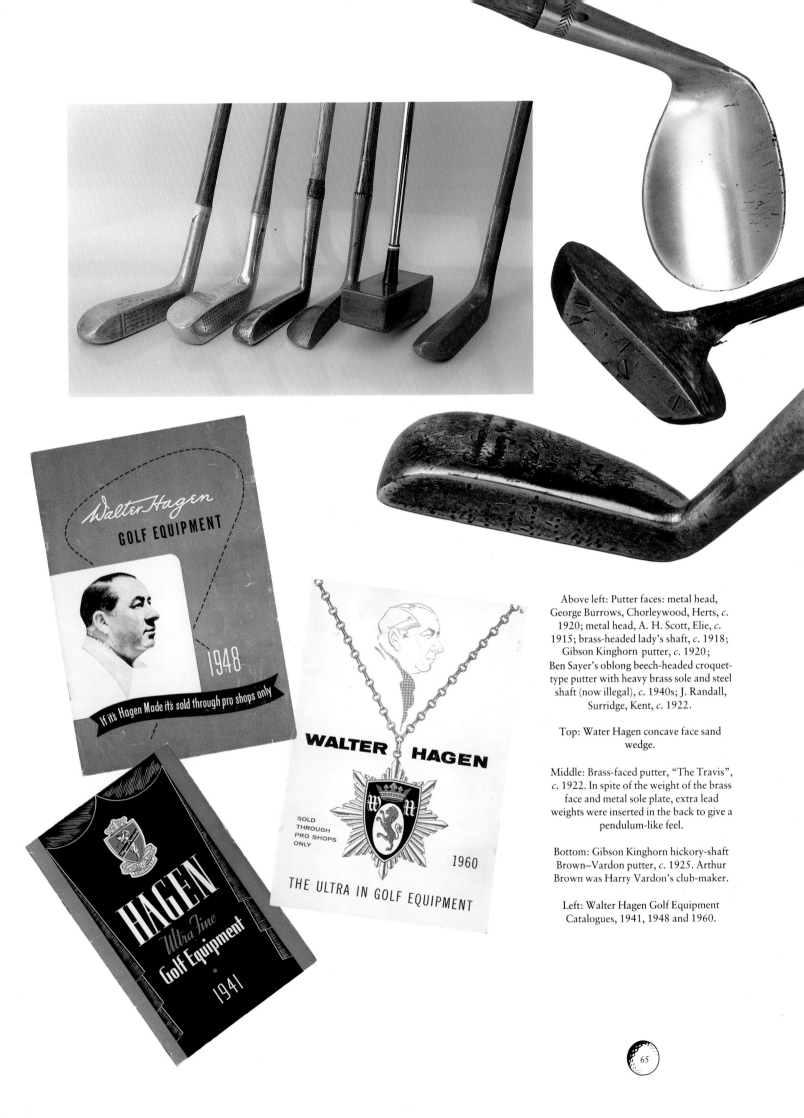

Above left: Putter faces: metal head, George Burrows, Chorleywood, Herts, *c.* 1920; metal head, A. H. Scott, Elie, *c.* 1915; brass-headed lady's shaft, *c.* 1918; Gibson Kinghorn putter, *c.* 1920; Ben Sayer's oblong beech-headed croquet-type putter with heavy brass sole and steel shaft (now illegal), *c.* 1940s; J. Randall, Surridge, Kent, *c.* 1922.

Top: Water Hagen concave face sand wedge.

Middle: Brass-faced putter, "The Travis", *c.* 1922. In spite of the weight of the brass face and metal sole plate, extra lead weights were inserted in the back to give a pendulum-like feel.

Bottom: Gibson Kinghorn hickory-shaft Brown–Vardon putter, *c.* 1925. Arthur Brown was Harry Vardon's club-maker.

Left: Walter Hagen Golf Equipment Catalogues, 1941, 1948 and 1960.

Wooden clubs. (Bottom: to top): Harry Vardon Spalding scared head, *c.* 1920; Philedia golf studio driver, *c.* 1920; W. Kane special Bulgar brassie; Spalding Dundee driver, *c.* 1920s.

complete smear, a difference in direction of sixty or eighty yards. It is extremely important at just what split-second of time the club head reaches the ball. So weight and balance among the clubs used must play a big part in timing. He may use a light club where he can have the feel of the head or a heavy club where he can't, and the difference will be marked when he begins swinging. The same is true of the lie of the club. A "flat lie" means a wider angle formed by shaft and club head and is used when one stands well away from the ball.

An "upright lie" means a smaller angle between shaft and club head and is suitable only when one stands closer to the ball. Otherwise the toe of the club will be well off the ground in either case. The lie of the club should be such that when the golfer takes his natural, normal stance the bottom of the club should be upon the ground without having the toe of the club in the air. Those golfers who are standing well away from the ball should use clubs with flatter lies. Those who are accustomed to playing closer to the ball should use the more upright variety and the selection of the right club in this respect is worth some study and attention. Otherwise the player will be hitting the ball with either the heel of the club or only half the toe.

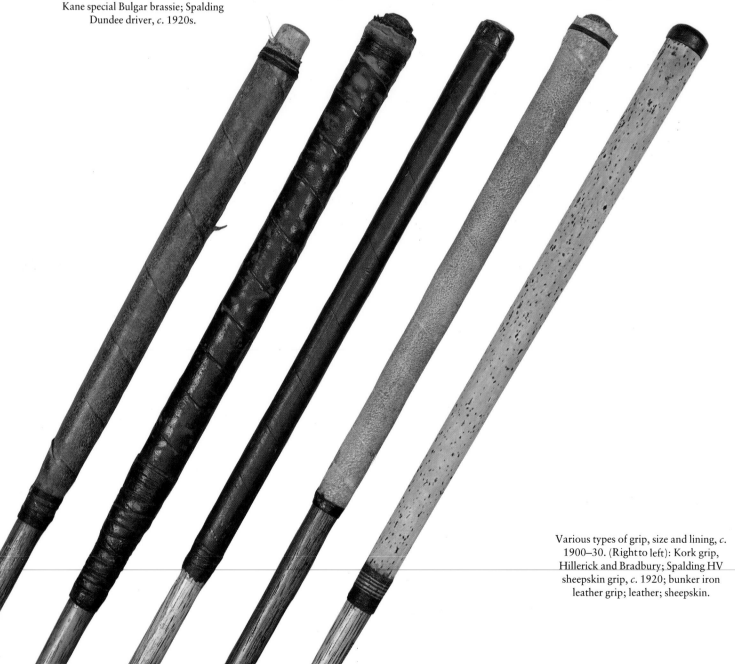

Various types of grip, size and lining, *c.* 1900–30. (Right to left): Kork grip, Hillerick and Bradbury; Spalding HV sheepskin grip, *c.* 1920; bunker iron leather grip; leather; sheepskin.

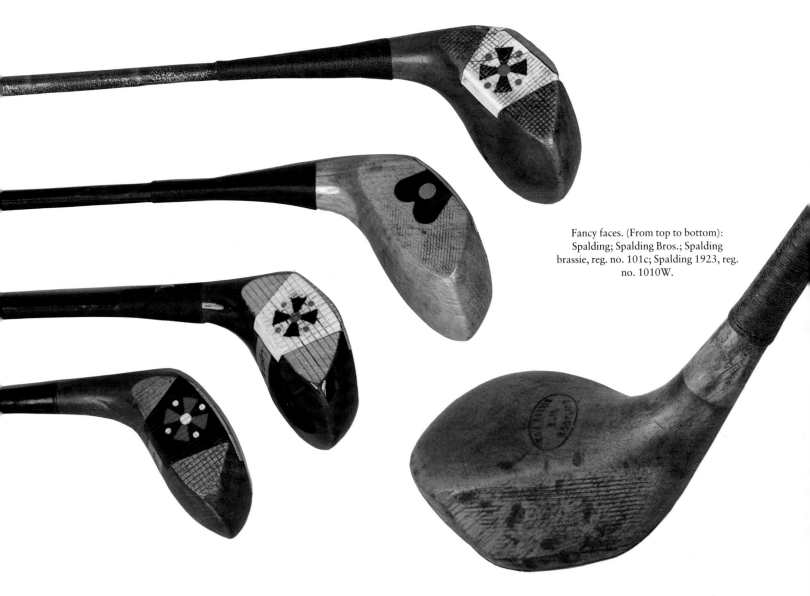

Fancy faces. (From top to bottom): Spalding; Spalding Bros.; Spalding brassie, reg. no. 101c; Spalding 1923, reg. no. 1010W.

"Pretty faces". (From bottom): A. J. reach, 7EB brassie; Walter Hagen Starline with aluminium firing pin; Spalding J. Medal 3 wooden dowl; St. Andrews Golf Company; Lynchometer; McGregor Master driver Patent 1922.

The Matter of Weight and Balance

In a game as delicately adjusted as golf is where feel, touch, timing, balance, etc. are of such deep importance it is easy enough to see the big part the club itself must play – the size of the grip – the weight and balance – the lie of the club head – the length – and other factors which must be considered. In the first place there is the size of the grip to be considered. And since the grip rests largely in the fingers, it should not be too large unless one has abnormally large hands or abnormally long fingers.

But probably one of the most important factors is the feel is the club head attached to a strong, firm shaft that isn't too bulky. After all there are not enough golfers who think about the club head in relation to the swing. You hit with the club head, and it is important to think about the clubhead. So it is important to feel the clubhead, otherwise one might as well be using a stick of wood. There should be a distinct, well balanced feel, but one can have too much weight at the end of the shaft and then control becomes tangled.

It is even more important that the iron clubs, midiron, mashie iron, mashie and mashie niblick have proper weight, balance and feel. Every golfer knows what it means to suddenly come upon an iron club that has the feeling of a perfect shot, the balance that just suits. If he can get possession of a club of this sort he is sure to play it with greater confidence and an offer of $50 wouldn't even tempt him. The mistake

Club faces. (Right to left): waffle face; mesh ball face; Spalding Crowfly Waterfall; McGregor backspin mashie; Wilsonian mashie; Spalding Crowflight; McGill medal mashie niblick; Diamond mid-iron, combined brick face and deep groove.

Ladies Clubs from a Wilson Golf Catalogue *c.*1927.

is often made of having too much weight in the blade of an iron club or too much wood in the shaft where the bulky heaviness of the entire club is covered up.

Where one usually makes the mistake is sampling ten or fifteen clubs in a store or shop and finally losing all sense of touch. It is usually a mistake to get an iron club with a flat lie. In playing a mashie or mashie niblick better results are found by standing closer to the ball than most golfers stand, and this calls for a rather upright lie.

Frequently the shaft begins to go before one knows what has happened and this also must be watched. The slower swinging golfer can use a trifle more whip in the shaft than a faster swinger and a harder hitter. There must be a general feeling of balance among all clubs. It is a mistake to have heavy wooden clubs and light irons; or heavy irons and light wooden clubs. One is more likely to have the clubs too long and too heavy rather than to have them too short and too light.

One is inclined to hurry the back swing of a club that is too light, but if there is the distinct touch of weight in the head it will help in slowing down the swing. Points to remember are not to have the grip too large, the club too long and too heavy, the shaft too bulky; but to have a feeling of balance, a feel of the club head and the right lie.

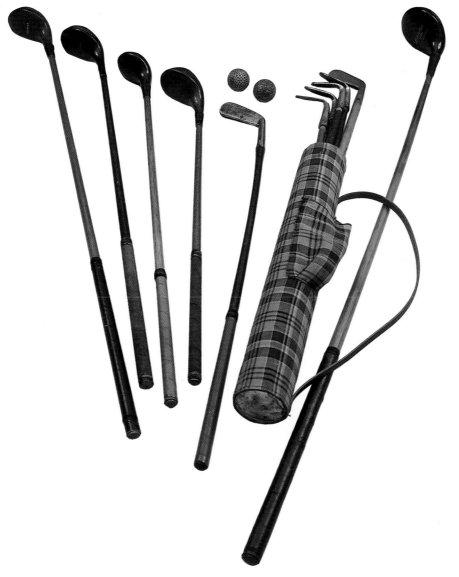

Miscellaneous children's clubs with golf game of clubs, with bag and balls. Full-size driver shows the size.

An Osmonds golf caddie bag.

GOLF BAGS

There are few hard and fast facts about the origins of golf, and the history of the game goes back too far for anyone to be able to date many aspects of its development with any accuracy. Of some things we can, however, be sure: first, that the game could not be played without three essential elements – a club, a ball and a patch of open land – and secondly, that the carrying of the clubs is possibly the one feature that has always marred the players' enjoyment of the game. Even in the very early days, pictorial evidence suggests that those who could afford a caddie employed one, sometimes to the extent of engaging him to tote two bundles of clubs around the links. Usually the player or his caddie tucked the "set" of clubs beneath his arm, with the heads of the clubs pointing towards the ground to provide balance.

There was obviously room for a receptacle to ease this chore, and it was probably the basket-weavers and similar craftsmen who hit upon the idea of making a wicker carrier. By the 1870s inventors were tinkering with strapping and strips of wood to make holders that would carry from five to eight clubs with little additional weight for the caddie.

Women's

VASSAR

R606. Women's Custom Built Vassar Golf Outfit. A particularly fine quality 6-club outfit especially designed for women. The Vassar driver and brassie are made with mahogany finished persimmon heads, attractive black and white fancy faces, alumo back weights and sole plates, chromium plated True Temper steel shafts and black calfskin bell top tapered grips with end caps. Vassar midiron, mashie, mashie niblic and putter are made with chromium plated heads, Wilson no-shock hosels and black adapters, chromium plated seamless drawn steel shafts and black grips. The bag is of pearl color elk hide with red cowhide trim, deep cuffs, hookless fastener on ball pocket and metal cup bottom.
Outfit Complete.....................$60.00

SUPER STROKE

R706. Women's De Luxe Super Stroke 6-club Golf Outfit is built especially for women golfers. The graceful fancy face steel shaft Ladies' Super Stroke Driver and Brassie and steel shafted Midiron, Mashie, Mashie Niblic and Putter made with chromium plated heads have been especially designed to meet the woman's golfing requirements. The special women's De Luxe Bag of waterproof tan suedetex is trimmed with a harmonizing snake skin and is equipped with padded sling, cushion top and bottom and hookless fastener on ball pocket.
Outfit Complete.....................$56.00

34

Golf Outfits

VOGUE

R804. Women's Vogue Golf Outfit, efficient in every sense of the word, has been planned with a careful regard to color harmony between the clubs and bag. The graceful business-like brassie is made with fancy face and steel shaft, and the hickory shafted midiron, mashie and putter are made with chromium plated heads. The special women's bag is of grey English Service Cloth with green trim, deep cuffs with white trim, padded sling strap, cushion top and bottom and hookless fastener on ball pocket.
Outfit Complete.....................$22.50

SMART SET

R904. Ladies' Smart Set Golf Outfit is ideal for the woman who plays occasionally. The clubs and bag have been designed to meet women's requirements and the entire set has been built in a color harmony that will appeal to every woman. Consists of special women's plain face steel shaft brassie and hickory shafted midiron, mashie and putter, made with chromium plated iron, mashie and putter, made with chromium plated heads. The waterproof grey whipcord bag is trimmed in blue and is equipped with padded sling strap, metal bottom and hookless fastener on ball pocket.
Outfit Complete.....................$17.50

35

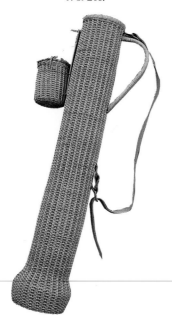

Unusual wicker basket summer golf bag, *c.* 1920s.

These club carriers eventually increased in scope and size, and during the early 1890s two companies were producing "stand-up" bags, which consisted of fold-away legs, leather or wood handles and a tubular canvas pouch as a compact container for clubs and accessories. By 1892 a caddie cart had been invented – a canvas tube with handle, straps, ball pocket and two small wheels attached to the base of the bag.

As golf clubs and societies grew in numbers, so too did the collection of clubs considered necessary to aid the players' game, and with them the sizes and styles of golf bags.

By the First World War, canvas bags reinforced with leather were being manufactured to hold any number of clubs from five to twenty. During 1920 and 1921, one manufacturer produced a 4½ in. ring bag from surplus army webbing and buckles left over from the 1914–18 war. This strong but surprisingly lightweight bag lasted for many years until fashion decreed its demise.

The larger bags were fitted with one or two pockets, a sturdy strap to tighten around the bag when it was being transported, and a shoulder strap which could be adjusted to balance a full complement of clubs, according to the caddie's or the golfer's height. Hoods were sewn to the top of the bag.

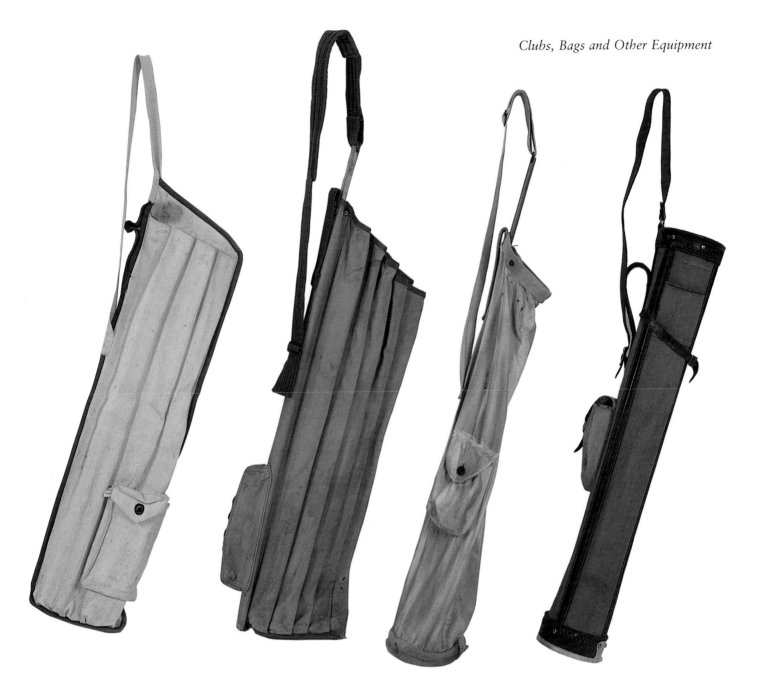

Four "Sunday" golf bags, *c.* 1914.

These would cover the clubs in inclement weather, and could be stowed within the bag in good conditions. However, the buckles of these hoods did much damage to the grips and shafts of wooden-shafted clubs. Steel supports were sewn into the sides of the larger bags, an innovation which provided the players with a quick and easy selection of clubs, as the bag stood upright.

Between the wars, the zip fastener transformed golf bags, and at least fifteen major companies vied with one another to produce the lightest, "swankiest" and most functional bag for professional or amateur, male or female players. As a matter of interest, the following are a few of the prices charged for golf bags from 1897 onwards: 1897 self-action bag with grasshopper tripod legs, 11*s*. 6*d*.; 1900 canvas 3½ inch (inside) ring pencil or Sunday bag, 5*s*. 6*d*.; 1905 cowhide 3½ inch (inside) ring pencil or Sunday bag with slot for umbrella, 12*s*. 6*d*.; 1912 canvas 5½ inch ring bag, 17*s*. 6*d*., with hood 3*s*. 6*d*. extra; 1912 calfskin 6½ inch ring bag, 75*s*. 6*d*.; 1922 canvas bag, ring or oval, 21*s*.; 1922 cowhide bag, ring or oval, 35*s*.; 1932 calfskin or hide 6 inch ring or oval, 90*s*.

LEATHER GOLF BAGS

8417. Men's finest quality all leather stayless bag. Genuine pearl elk hide body with genuine tan cowhide trim and deep cuffs. Tan leather lacing around cuffs and pockets increases the attractive appearance of the bag. All hardware including special locks similar to those illustrated is of polished brass. The bag is equipped with club separating and utility straps, form fitting pitcher handle, padded Kaddy Komfort sling strap and cushion bottom. Shoe pocket, roomy ball pocket and cowhide hood are equipped with hookless fasteners, as is full length opening down side of bag. 7-inch diameter....................Each, $45.00

8427. Men's all leather stayless bag, exactly the same as 8417 except made of black calfskin throughout. Ea., $45.00

8407. Men's all leather stayless bag, exactly the same as 8417 except made with tan body and pearl trim. Ea., $45.00

8327. Men's high quality all leather seven-inch stayless bag. A sturdy model in the more conservative style, made of genuine black cowhide throughout. White lacing around the heavy cuffs and the pockets adds just the right touch of color. Equipped with club separating, umbrella and utility straps, comfortable pitcher handle, padded Kaddy Komfort sling strap and cushion bottom. All hardware, including special locks similar to those illustrated, is polished brass. The shoe pocket and ball pockets and the leather hood are equipped with the popular hookless fasteners....................Each, $42.50

8307. A beautiful all leather stayless bag exactly the same in design and construction as the 8327, except that it is pearl color throughout....................Each, $42.50

8317. Men's coffee color all leather stayless bag, built to the same design and construction specifications as the 8327....................Each, $42.50

8217. Men's high quality heavy coffee color genuine cowhide 7-inch stayless bag, tan laced around cuffs and pocket. Kaddy Komfort sling strap, pitcher handle, club separating, utility and umbrella straps and cushion bottom. Hookless fasteners on large ball pocket and hood. Special locks similar to those illustrated....................Each, $38.50

8207. Men's genuine cowhide bag, exactly the same as 8217 except pearl color....................Each, $38.50

8227. Men's genuine cowhide bag, exactly the same as 8217 except black....................Each, $38.50

7407. Men's high quality golden tan color genuine cowhide 7-inch stayless bag. Made with heavy cuffs, pitcher handle, Kaddy Komfort sling, utility and club separating straps and cushion bottom. Equipped with hookless fasteners on ball and clothing pockets, hood and on full length opening on side of bag. Each....................$32.50

7417. Men's genuine cowhide stayless bag, exactly the same as 7407, except black....................Each, $32.50

7427. Men's genuine cowhide stayless bag, exactly the same as 7407, except pearl color....................Each, $32.50

7347. Men's high quality pearl color genuine cowhide 7-in. stayless bag. Made with padded Kaddy Komfort sling strap, comfortable pitcher handle, club separating and utility strap and cushion bottom. Large shoe and ball pockets and hood equipped with hookless fasteners. Each......$30.00

7337. All leather bag, same as 7347 except brown....Each, $30.00

7327. All leather bag, same as 7347, except black....Each, $30.00

Selection from *The Gateway to Golf*, a complete catalogue of Wilson Golf equipment for 1931.

Opposite: Selection of golf tees, mainly American, 1915–30.

By 1932 bags had divisions to separate the clubs, with larger partitions to divide the woods from the irons, then quarter partitions, and finally plastic tubes for each club, to prevent chafing of club grips. Following the Second World War, there was some delay before materials such as leather, canvas and steel became sufficiently plentiful for manufacturers to return to full production. During the war years, however, a greater variety of man-made materials had been developed which could be used to complement or replace leather, and by the early 1950s competitive golfers were sporting huge golf bags which certainly required a trolley, if not a cart to carry them.

Despite the Royal and Ancient's limiting the number of clubs to 14 in May 1939, there was no voluntary reduction in bag sizes by the manufacturers. Three, four or five pocket bags (incorporating the hood as a pocket) adorned the professionals' shops and showrooms, and by 1948 more and more trolleys were appearing on the courses. Half a century later, we look with bewilderment at the size and shape of the multi-coloured receptacles which come under the name of golf bags and which act as a veritable wardrobe to the player, who carries so many accessories. Who knows what the future holds for the pampered golfer? We now read of the remote-controlled caddie, through which "at the touch of a button" you can direct your trolley and bag to await you on any part of the fairway or teeing ground. Is this the death knell for the caddie?

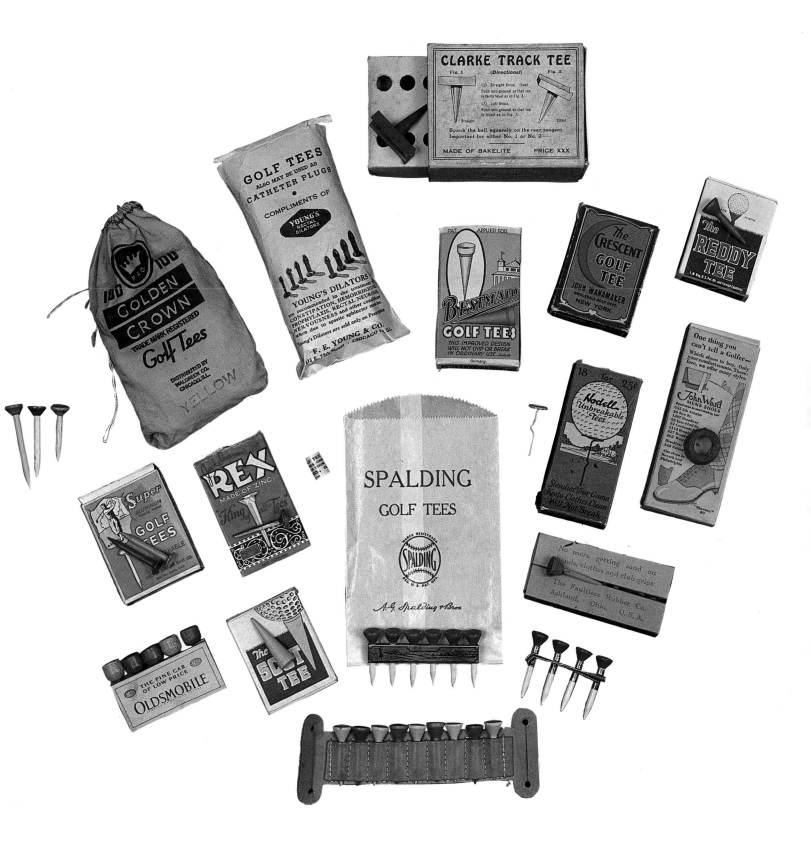

OTHER EQUIPMENT

Apart from balls, clubs and bags, there are many other golfing accessories that are much in demand by collectors today. The wooden tee is commonplace now, but up to the 1940s the peg-type was still widely used. In the beginning tees were formed with a small mound of sand or dirt from special band tee boxes and brass or metal tee moulds were used. More and more manufacturers experimented with different materials and shapes and their results are very collectible. Ransome's, for example, made a double gold tee stamp or mould in polished brass in around 1890. It cost 1*s*. and came in two different heights of tee.

PROVISIONAL SPECIFICATION.

Improvements in Moulds for Shaping Sand "Tees" used in the Game of Golf.

FREDERICK WILLIAM WAREING, 5, Windsor Place, Fleetwood, Lancashire, Civil and Mechanical Engineer, do hereby declare the nature of this invention to be as follows:–

My present invention relates to a means of providing golf players with an apparatus whereby a "sand tee" can be easily & expeditiously formed without handling the damp sand, or soiling the fingers & thereby ensuring regularity of height of the "tee." I am aware that there is a "tee" mould in existence for this purpose, but my invention differs from this by the use of a spring side in order to obviate the tendency of the sand to adhere to the sides of the mould.

In order to further facilitate the sand leaving the mould, I have a small opening in or near the top of the mould so as to allow the air to escape when filling the mould with sand & also ensure the ready escape of the moulded sand when the "tee" is being formed, I do not claim a specific size of mould.

Dated this 25th day of March 1898.

Selection of tees made in wood and plastic, showing a good cross-selection of advertising. Some tee cards include a score card. The "Colonel" paper tees with box are the earliest, *c*. 1905. Tin sand tee mould. Four tins of tape for the golfer by K. D. Manufacturing Company, Pennsylvania. The golf comparator is a cardboard aid for the golfer to look through and decide which club to select. All items date from 1905–40.

Packets of tees were often sold complete with a scorecard, so that they looked like match books. Practice aids of all kinds can still be found, as can golf course memorabilia such as hole cutters.

GREAT CHAMPIONS

Since the first Open Championship was held in 1860 certain golf players, both amateur and professional, have become household names. Television has made many of the present-day champions familiar even to non-playing audiences. The following list, which is given in order of the birth dates of those included, therefore concentrates on some of the outstanding golfers of the more distant past.

TOM MORRIS

Tom Morris Senior was born in St Andrews on 16 June 1821, the son of a postman. He became a caddie and was then apprenticed to Allan Robertson in 1839. After going to Prestwick for several years in 1851, he returned to St Andrews in 1865 to become greenkeeper to the Royal and Ancient Golf Club, a position he held until 1904.

On Sunday afternoon I saw Old Tom, "stravaigin'" over the Links. It was a brilliant Autumn afternoon; one felt exhilarated with every draught of the highly ozoned air from land and sea.

Of course, when on the Links, Sunday or Saturday, golfers cannot restrain the talk about the game. I certainly began by sympathising with my revered friend for the climax to his bereavements in the lamented death of his favourite child, Mrs. Hunter – his "Libby." In silence we walked on meditating, till all of a sudden he remarked: "That puttin' green cost me a lot o' trouble. I wud hae them to see an' keep in the

A CHAT WITH OLD TOM by J.G. McPherson, from *Golf*, 4 November 1898

Four cigarette cards. (From left to right): James Braid; Harry Vardon; Tom Morris Senior; John Ball.

Tom Morris in the doorway of his golf shop, *c.* 1885.

slicht ups and doons an' no mak' it like a green cloth table. But it was a' I cud dae to hud them in." "That is a fine rich turf, Tom," I remarked. "Aye, it's the saund." The sand is with Tom the cure for all links' diseases, and certainly on the occasion it seemed to drive away the reminiscences of his loss. When I made reference to this, he acknowledged that the "Links is my salvation."

He told me of the origin of his "saund" experiments: – The tenth hole at Prestwick was, forty years ago, in a bad state. Tom was then custodian of the links there. To save it from putting damage he shifted it a bit, and by accident some sand fell on a part of the putting green. This was rather strange, for then no sand was used for teeing – no sand boxes were on any course. In the spring Tom happened to "study" this relieved ground: and he observed that the grass was showing beautiful light green shoots through the sprinkled sand when no resuscitation was noticeable elsewhere. The thought, happily, struck him that the sand was the case of this growth. Accordingly, he took his big red handkerchief and filled it repeatedly from an adjoining bunker, and strewed the sand over the putting green. The recovery was magical, and from that day to this Tom has held on to the the marvellous recuperative powers of "saund" in natural coast greens.

Between 1861 and 1896 he competed in every Open Championship and won four times, in 1861, 1862, 1864 and 1867. Old Tom died in 1908. He was highly thought of and is commemorated by having the eighteenth green named after him at the Royal and Ancient and by a portrait hanging in the club house.

WILLIE PARK

In 1860 Willie Park was the first person to win the Challenge Belt (though no prize money) in a year when just eight professionals competed. He also won in 1863, 1866 and 1875. Park had begun as a caddie at Musselburgh and went on to excel at match play. He was well known for his characteristic pause at the top of his swing and for his accurate putting.

Willie Park Senior was born in Walleyford near Musselburgh in 1833. Shortly afterwards his family moved to a house by Musselburgh links and Willie began to carry clubs.

His first major match was against Tom Morris in 1854, when he won by five holes. The two men played many more historic matches together, although the most famous took place in 1871, when with six holes to play Willie was two strokes up and the referee stopped the match because the spectators were moving the balls. Tom Morris decided to go for some refreshment at Mrs Foreman's tavern and did not return. Willie completed the round alone in 21, with Tom completing the next day in 26.

Willie also made clubs. He is believed to have set up in business in 1853 making feathery golf balls. His early clubs were stamped "Wm Park" and were sold to the gentlemen of golfing clubs. Most of the clubs attributed to him are play clubs or drivers and made of wood. It is unlikely that he made any iron clubs at all. He employed apprentices to do the routine work, and before he retired in 1887 his son Willie Park Junior had joined him in the business. Willie Park died in 1903.

Left: Tom Morris from the original painting by Reed.

Right: Ainsley Ceramic Trophy 7 inches high. Handpainted by J. Shaw and the only one made. It shows Tom Morris at St. Andrews in about 1895.

MUNGO PARK

Born in 1839, Mungo Park, William's brother, spent his youth at sea. He won the championship in 1874 with a record score of 159, which remained unbroken until 1886. In the 1880s he began work as greenkeeper and professional at Alnmouth Golf Club, where there is a bunker named after him.

He made a very few clubs, marked "M. Park", between about 1875 and 1890. Though not as well-made as his brother's clubs, they are sought after today because he was an Open Champion.

TOM MORRIS JUNIOR

Born in St. Andrews in 1851, by the time he was 16 years old Tom Morris Junior had won the Open Professional Tournament at Montrose. He then went on to win the Championship Belt three times in successive years from 1868 to 1870 and was thus able to keep it. There was no Open in 1871, but in 1872 he won again, for the fourth time.

Tommy was a dashing golfer, usually playing in the typical Glengarry bonnet of the Scotch, and which generally fell from his head as he swung, very like Harold Hilton's cap. His hands and wrists were exceedingly powerful and he had been known to break the shaft of his driver, under the grip as he waggled in address. But as a putter he knew no equal. He stroked his putt off his right leg with the ball so close to his

Rare postcard showing Tom Morris and Tom Morris Junior, *c. 1905*.

"YOUNG TOM" MORRIS, PEERLESS GOLFER by A. W. Tillinghurst, from *Golf Illustrated*, June 1934

FOUNDER OF FIRM

TOM MORRIS

CHAMPION 1861-62, 64, 67

SON OF FOUNDER.

TOM MORRIS, JUNR.
(YOUNG TOMMY)

CHAMPION 1868-69, 70, 72.

WINNER OF CHAMPIONSHIP BELT AND 1st
CHAMPIONSHIP MEDAL

RECORD ST. ANDREWS COURSE, 1869 77 STROKES

right foot that it seemed that he must strike his toes. He half-topped his putts, which kept them rolling true to an astonishing extent. Of course, all great champions are great putters – at times as are we all, but generally they are consistently fine putters. It must be remarked that Tommy Morris was not only consistently good, but consistently *deadly*.

But apparently he had no weakness. His driving was sure and hard, and he could *press* if need be without going wild. With the irons he was master of all the shots from the quarter and half-irons up to the full shots, and like all St. Andrews' men he liked to play the low running approaches. Let us for a moment analyze his scoring in the four championships which he won at Prestwick. For the first three wins he averaged 76–2/3 strokes for each eighteen holes, and although his score in 1872 was higher and ran his average for the four championships up to 78–1/4 strokes, still his play was remarkable at a time when good scores were constantly in the eighties, playing with a solid ball of gutta percha.

It is significant that for nearly twenty years no Championship winner came within eight shots of Tommy's 149. As late as 1890 the Open Championship was won over the same Prestwick course by John Ball Jr., of the Royal Liverpool Club, with a total of 164. Tommy *was* great.

Young Tom Morris wearing his Championship Belt, *c*.1873.

Tom Morris Junior was undoubtedly the best golfer of his time, but the distressing death of his wife while he was playing with his father against Willie and Mungo Park at North Berwick had a very sad effect on him and he died on 25 December 1875, a few months after his wife, at the age of 24. A monument showing Young Tom in golfing attire can be seen in St. Andrews Cathedral churchyard.

JOHN BALL

John Ball was the first Englishman and the first amateur to break the Scottish stranglehold on the Open. He was born on 24 December 1863 in Hoylake, where his father owned the Royal Hotel. The race-course then at Hoylake was later to become the Royal Liverpool Golf Club. When he was just 15 Ball came sixth in the Open, although there was some doubt as to whether he should receive his prize money in case it affected his amateur status. Because of his talent and his age, however, this difficulty was overlooked. He first played in the Open in 1878 at the age of 17 and came fourth. He won the Amateur Championship eight times, in 1888, 1890, 1892, 1894, 1899, 1907, 1910 and 1912.

In 1890 he won both the Open and the British Amateur Championship, becoming the first of only two players to hold both titles in the same year (Bobby Jones achieved the same success in 1930). Ball served in the Boer War in 1899 and did not compete for three years.

The last Amateur Championship he played was in 1921, when the Americans were first beginning seriously to compete in Britain. He reached the fifth round although he was 58 years old. He retired to farm in Wales, where he died in December 1940.

A picture of Willie Park Jnr.

WILLIAM PARK JUNIOR

William Park Junior was born at Musselburgh in 1864. His early golfing days were spent at the Tyneside Golf Club, Rynton-on-Tyne. Having returned to Musselburgh in 1884, he competed in his first Open the following year, won in 1887 and 1889, and was runner-up to Harry Vardon in 1898. He then expanded his interests to include golf architecture, writing and club-making. Like his father, he was a teetotaller. Park wrote two important books, *The Game of Golf* (1896), which can be regarded as the first instructional book of golf, and *The Art of Putting* (1920). He died in 1925.

EMINENT GOLFERS: WILLIE PARK JUN. by Fred W. M. Kitto, from *Golf*, 12 June 1891

"Ye're no worth a preen if ye dinna keep cool." Few professional golfers are so universally liked as Willie Park, and we may say with truth that he is a man without a single enemy. The game of Golf is indebted to him for the introduction of three new clubs, all of which are widely used. Thousands use the "Lofter" and "Patent Cleek," and who has not heard of the "Bulger," the cure for all faults of driving? Though this concealer of "heel and toe" disease does not bear his name, still it was his brain that conceived it and his hand that fashioned the first "bulger." It may astonish some to hear how very little practice Willie Park requires in order to get into form. He, perhaps, plays less Golf than any other professional. He has not "touched a club" since playing at St. Anne's in November, nor will he do so, probably, until the tournaments come on again, when he will take a short holiday of a fortnight or so. During this time he does nothing but play Golf, and the effect of this practice is generally felt by his opponents. Such, briefly, are the doings of Willie Park, Jun., truly a good record.

The Parks, father and son, also played a very influential part in the development of clubs and balls. William Park Junior is reputed to have invented and manufactured the bulger club in 1884 and the lofter club in 1888. He expanded the business into a number of different sites and advertised extensively, often taking out more space in the journals than his competitors. The Parks' company specialized at first in patented clubs, but by the end of the nineteenth century it was employing around seventy people making all kinds of golf equipment. The clubs were all hand-made, and the Parks did not take kindly to new ideas of mass production.

Willie Park Junior designed many patterns for moulded gutta percha balls, the most famous of which is the Park "Royal", patented in 1894, with its hexagonally faced surface. Two other well-known balls from his factory are the "Dispatch" and the "Times". He also designed over a hundred golf courses in great Britain, the United States and Canada. Of these, the most noteworthy include Seaford, Gullane and Sunningdale.

As an afterthought, it is worth mentioning Willie Park's caddie, who was almost as famous as he was, and became known as "Fiery".

HAROLD HILTON

Harold Hilton was born in Kirby on 12 January 1869. He won the Open Championship in 1892 when the Championship was extended to seventy-two holes, and again in 1897; and won the Irish Open Championship and the Amateur Championship four times each. He held the US and British Amateur titles in the same year, being the first player and the only Briton to do so.

A writer of books, he was the first editor of *Golf Monthly* until 1914 when war broke out. He died on 5 March 1942.

Cigarette card of Harold Hilton.

Cigarette cards from a series of 100 by Gallaher Ltd, showing James Braid with tips for good playing. (From left to right): No. 3, stance, address and position of ball for a full drive or brassey shot; No. 4, address for a cleek shot when playing against the wind; No. 8, stance and address for bunker stroke with niblick; No. 5, top of the swing for full drive or brassey shot (front view).

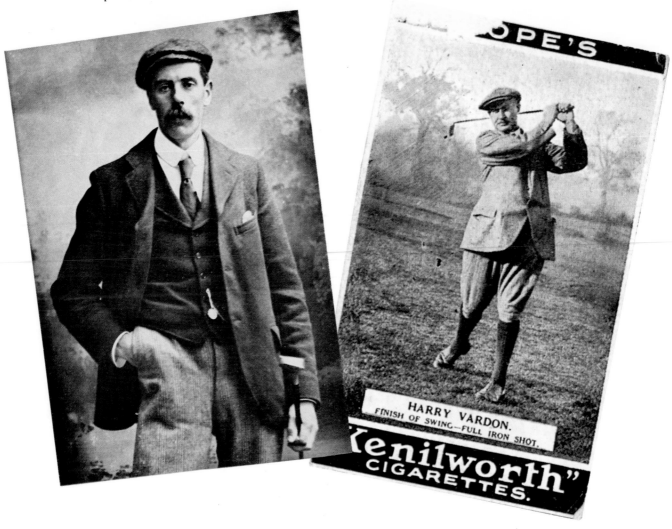

Left: James Braid.

Right: Harry Vardon on Cope's Kenilworth cigarette card, *c*.1912.

JAMES BRAID

James Braid was born in Elie, Fife, on 6 February 1870. An acknowledged master of golf, he was one of the three men known as "the great triumvirate", together with J. H. Taylor and Harry Vardon, since they exercised an important influence on the game for twenty years before the First World War. Braid was the first golfer to win the Open Championship five times, in 1901 and 1906 at Muirfield, in 1905 and 1910 at St. Andrews and in 1908 at Prestwick. Taylor later equalled this record and Vardon went on to win the Open Championship six times.

Having played as an amateur in Fife and Edinburgh, in 1893 Braid went to London, where he found employment as a club-maker. He turned professional in 1896. In a memorable foursome, Braid paired with Alex Herd lost to Harry Vardon and John Taylor in a match over four courses with a prize of £400.

GOLF HEROES OF
OTHER DAYS:
JAMES BRAID by
Bernard Darwin,
*from The American
Golfer*, January
1935

Certainly no man ever played golf with a wiser head, though I have heard him say that he liked to feel just a wee bit nervous before starting. Oddly enough he combined with this quality a power of hitting at the ball with an almost reckless abandon as if he meant to kill it. He would march along the course with a long, slow, almost sleepy stride and then when he came to the ball he would lash at it with what

Mr. Horace Hutchinson well called a "divine fury"; and indeed, though one must write of his triumphs in the past tense, he can still do so.

He was a superb iron player, famous especially with the now departed cleek, a master of every kind of running shot, and though not naturally a good putter he made himself for one period of his career almost a great one. A better player out of difficulties I am sure was never seen, for not only could he by pure strength remove tons of sand and acres of heather, but he was as skilful and resourceful as he was strong. In fact at his best, he was almost impregnably armed at all points, but it was his driving that delighted people when he first appeared and it is still his driving, more especially against the wind, that they remember best. It was at once so appalling in its ferocity, so rhythmical in its majesty.

Braid may almost be said to have inherited long driving, since he was a cousin of Douglas Rolland who came like him from Elie in Fife and was the legendary long driver of the "eighties" and early "nineties." He himself has given to the world the mysterious piece of natural history that he went to bed one night a short driver and woke up next morning a long one. We must take his word for it, but I never heard of anyone who remembered him as a short driver, and he assuredly was a long one, when, with something of the suddenness of a meteor, he flashed upon the golfing world about 1895.

Braid was a tall man and a powerful player who rarely lost his temper. He was a founder member of the Professional Golfers Association. After being the professional at Romford for eight years and at Walton Heath for forty-five years, he was made an honorary member of Walton Heath for twenty-five years. Braid was also a golf course architect and was greatly admired for his influence on the game. He died in London in 1950.

Left: Harry Vardon driving off, 1903.

Right: Tom Morris, Harry Vardon and Alex Herd, *c*.1903.

THE OLD
MASTERS: HARRY
VARDON by
Bernard Darwin,
from *The American
Golfer*, October
1929

Left: St. Andrews First Hole and Swilcan
Burn, 1904.

Right: J. H. Taylor driving off with Tom
Morris in the background at the Open
Championship, St. Andrews 1903.

I am not going to argue as to whether or not Vardon is the greatest golfer that ever lived. These comparisons are futile. It is enough that he was *the* golfer of his time. He won the British Open Championship in 1896, 1898, 1899, 1903, 1911 and 1914; he won the American Championship in 1900. He was probably at his very best in 1898 and 1899 before his visit to America. In point of health and strength he was not quite the same man afterwards and he himself has said that he thinks he left a little of his game there. It was not till some little time later that his actual and very serious illness developed and he won two more Championships after he was well again, but never again did he show the same utterly crushing superiority, which caused Andrew Kirkaldy to say that he would break the heart of an iron ox.

Of the "triumvirate" – Vardon, Braid and Taylor – Taylor is actually the youngest by a few months, but he was the first to make his name. He leaped into fame in 1893 when he began knocking down the big men like ninepins and in both 1894 and 1895 he was champion. Very few people had heard of Harry Vardon then, nobody perhaps save a few golfers in the north of England who had backed him in a home-to-home match against Sandy Herd and seen him badly beaten. In the winter of 1895–96 half a dozen leading professionals were asked to go out to play at Pau; someone of discerning judgment made Vardon one of the party and the rest of the world asked "who is this fellow Vardon?"

Then in the spring of 1896 Taylor, twice the champion, played Vardon on his home course at Ganton in Yorkshire and came away beaten by a pocketful of holes and declared that here was the man that he feared most in the coming championship. It was a sound piece of prophecy for the two tied at Muirfield and Vardon won on playing off. In the next year the new star waned a little and then in 1898 blazed out in full glory.

For the next two years, if Vardon was in the field no one looked any further for the winner; he crushed everyone; he once beat Taylor at Newcastle in Ireland by 12 and 11 and Taylor was playing his game. In 1900 he went to America and after that he was, right up till the war, one of the two or three unquestioned best, but he was never again, as he had been, in a completely different class from all the other golfers.

BERNARD DARWIN

The grandson of naturalist Charles Darwin, Bernard was born in Kent in 1876. He was educated at Eton and Trinity College, Cambridge, where he captained the golf side in 1897. As well as playing in international matches from 1902 to 1924, including the first Walker Cup tournament in 1922, he also began writing about the game in 1907 for *Country Life* and went on to complete over twenty-five books. The foremost golf writer of his day, he knew all the top golfers of his time and had a wonderful memory for courses. He was awarded the CBE for services to literature and sport in 1937 and died in 1961 at the age of 85.

Bernard Darwin, captain elect of the Royal and Ancient Golf Club, 1934–5, with the President's putter, from *Golf Monthly*, 1936.

Second Shots: Casual Talks about Golf, by Bernard Darwin. Two versions with different dust-covers, 1930. The yellow cover is said to have been illustrated by Darwin's wife Elinor Monsell, and Darwin is the figure peeping out of the bottom right-hand corner.

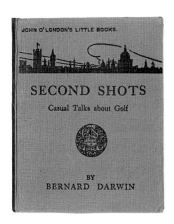
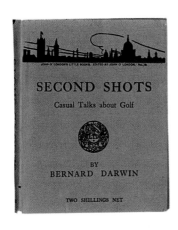
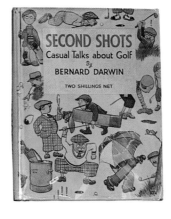
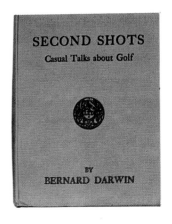

Gum card showing Walter Hagen.

WALTER HAGEN

Walter Hagen was born in Rochester, New York, in 1892. He was Open Champion in 1922, 1924, 1928 and 1929, United States Open Champion in 1914 and 1919, American PGA Champion in 1921, 1924, 1925, 1926 and 1927, played in the Ryder Cup in 1927, 1929, 1931, 1933 and 1935, and non-playing captain in 1937. He was well known for his flamboyant style of dressing. In earlier days, professionals were not allowed to enter the clubhouse so Hagen hired a Rolls Royce to use as a changing room and employed a butler to serve him a lavish meal. He liked to live like a millionaire. Very relaxed in his attitude, he would often talk to spectators in between shots and advised players to "Take time to smell the flowers." A very popular golfer, he was known as "The Haig". In 1956 he wrote *The Walter Hagen Story*. He died in 1969.

CYRIL TOLLEY

Cyril Tolley was born in 1896. A major figure in amateur golf, he won the first of his amateur championships in 1920 while still a student at Oxford University, and continued to represent his country until 1938. He was the only amateur ever to win the French Open twice, in 1924 and 1929. In the 1930 British Open, he played with Bobby Jones in the fourth round, which Jones won with a stymie at the 19th hole. He was elected captain of the Royal and Ancient Golf Club in 1948. In 1924 he wrote *The Modern Golfer*, which was partly instructional and partly a book of reminiscences. He died in 1978.

GENE SARAZEN

Gene Sarazen was born in 1902 in Hanson, New York. He was American PGSA Champion in 1922, 1923 and 1933, British Open Champion in 1932, United States Open Champion in 1922 and 1933, Masters Champion in 1935 and made Ryder Cup appearances in 1927, 1929, 1931, 1933, 1935 and 1937.

In 1973 the Royal and Ancient Golf Club invited all past winners to compete. Although Sarazen was then 71 years old, in the first round he had a hole in one at the famous Postage Stamp, the eighth hole at Troon. As if this was not dramatic enough, in the second round he holed a bunker shot for a two at the same hole.

Famous for always wearing plus-fours, Sarazen invented the famous sand-wedge and wrote several books, including *Commonsense Golf Tips* in 1924, and *Thirty years of Championship Golf: The Life and Times of Gene Sarazen* in 1950 together with Herbert Warren Wind. This last is one of the most interesting books and a corner stone in any golfer's library.

ROBERT (BOBBY) TYRE JONES JUNIOR

Bob Jones, as he preferred to be called, was a legend in his lifetime and achieved enormous success in the space of eight years. During his career he won the Open Championship in 1926, 1927 and 1930; the Amateur Championship in 1930; the United States Open in 1923, 1926, 1929 and 1930; the United States Amateur Championship in 1924, 1925, 1927, 1928 and 1930; and the Walker Cup in 1922, 1924, 1926, 1928 and 1930. In 1930, having won the Grand Slam at the age of 28, he immediately retired.

Left: Senior Service cigarette card of Bobby Jones, No 19 in 'Sporting Events and Stars' series of 96.

Middle: Stamps issued to commemorate Bobby Jones in 1981.

Right: J. Millhoff cigarette card of Bobby Jones, No. 20, from 'Famous Golfers' series of 27 cards.

GOLF - R. T. (BOBBY) JONES. U.S.A

BOBBY JONES
WINS THE OPEN
by E. M. Adams,
from *Golfers
Magazine*, August
1929

Left: Churchman's cigarette card of
Bobby Jones.

Bobby Jones when he sailed with the
Walker Cup team for England on the
Mauretania, 1927.

Spalding Golf Guide for 1931. Cover
shows Bobby Jones with his four major
trophies.

Now, the hero of our story has built up a record of victories in Open and Amateur events that has stamped him the world's greatest golfer – and rightly so, for there never has been and possibly never will be another Bobby Jones. We are all willing to concede that Jones is the master golfer of all time and yet we wonder if the golfing public realizes just wherein his greatness lies. Insofar as individual shots are concerned, we could name many players who are his equal, but not one of them, with the exception of Walter Hagen, can continue to play perfect shots under adverse conditions.

Bobby makes mistakes, for after all he is only human, but he knows how to recover from tough situations and he is never at a loss as to what to do next. Where other players become nervous and temperamental, he keeps his head, studies the lie of his ball carefully and the effect of this mental attitude on his game has made Jones the greatest of them all. Bobby did not always possess this ideal temperament; it was something he had to work hard to acquire and that we believe is the foundation of his supremacy.

Jones's recent victory in the National Open at the Winged Foot Golf Club, Mamaroneck, New York, gave him his third title in the event. There was a thirty-six hole play-off for the title and the crushing defeat that Bobby meted out to Al Espinosa is more like fiction than fact. There was Jones, playing machine-like golf,

scoring rounds of 72–69 for a total of 141, while Espinosa, shooting to the rough, landing in traps, and missing short putts, rolled up cards of 84–80, a miserable total of 164.

Findlay S. Douglas, president of the United States Golf Association, presented the Championship trophy and golf medal to Bobby Jones on the terrace in front of the Winged Foot Clubhouse. Cameramen and the movie tone recorded the event while members of the faithful gallery listened to the speeches and cheered the victor. At the conclusion of the presentation, the club members, led by Fred Ryan, sang "Hail to the Wingèd Foot," in honor of Bobby Jones.

Born on 17 March 1902 in Atlanta, Georgia, Bob Jones was a sickly child and not expected to live long. He was allergic to most foods, but gradually overcame this disability and took up sports. His home was near the East Lake course of the Atlantic Athletic Club, and there he met the professional, Stewart Maiden, who recognized his talent. Maiden made no attempt to alter Jones's natural swing. Indeed, Jones never actually had a golf lesson.

A highly sensitive but unassuming person, Jones had quite a temper, which he learned to control. When playing in tournaments it was not unusual for him to lose up to 14 lb in weight. He wrote his first book, *Down the Fairway*

Bobby Jones on Golf, first edition, 1926.

Time Magazine cover, March 1952, showing Robert Tyre Jones. Copyright 1952 Time Warner Inc. Reprinted by permission.

Golfing magazine cover, April 1960, with Bobby Jones.

Photograph of Bobby Jones about 7 years old at the top of his swing. In April 1930 Bobby Jones said it was pretty much like the top of his swing today as far as he could tell. USGA Photograph Library.

Opposite, above: The USGA Ben Hogan trophy, awarded each year by the Golf Writers' Association of America to the golfer making the greatest comeback from a physical disability. Established in 1953 by Robert A. Hudson, it has been won by Babe Zaharias in 1953, Dwight Eisenhower in 1955 and Patty Berg in 1974.

Opposite right: *Time Magazine* cover, January 1949, showing Ben Hogan. Copyright 1949 Time Warner Inc. Reprinted by permission.

Opposite far right: Sam Snead Golf cigarette card.

in 1927 when he was 25. Golf was not his whole life, and he already had a mechanical engineering degree from Georgia Technical College and an English literature degree from Harvard. He passed his law finals in just two years and entered his father's legal practice. He wrote *Bobby Jones on Golf* in 1930, *Golf Is My Game* in 1960, and several articles for *The American Golfer*. He made a film with Warner Brothers entitled *How I Play Golf*.

After his retirement he continued to be actively involved in golf and it was his dream to build the ideal course, suitable for both professional and lay players. It was at Interlachen in 1930, after he had won the United States Open, that he began to look for a location. He had decided to work with Dr Alister Mackenzie, the Scottish architect. They found Fruitlands, which was to become the famous Augusta National, although sadly Mackenzie died before the course was completed.

Bobby had to stop playing in 1948, as he was plagued by muscle problems which forced him to wear a leg brace and to undergo several operations. Eventually he was diagnosed as suffering from syryngomyelia, an extremely rare illness, and in the end was confined to a wheelchair.

In 1958 Bob Jones was non-playing captain of the first World Team Championships, and at the same time he received the freedom of the city of St. Andrews. He was only the second United States citizen to be so honoured, the previous recipient being Benjamin Franklin in 1757. Jones died in 1972.

HENRY COTTON

Henry Cotton was born in London on 26 January 1907 and became a professional golfer at the age of 17. He won the British Open at Royal St. George's, Sandwich, by five strokes in 1934, thus breaking a period of American domination of the game. His second round of sixty-five led Dunlop to rename their ball the "65". Cotton won the Open again in 1937 at Carnoustie and in 1948 at Muirfield, when he was 41 years old. No doubt if the war had not intervened he would have won many more titles.

After being invalided out of the Royal Air Force he took part in exhibition matches to raise money for the Red Cross. He played in the 1929, 1937 and 1947 Ryder Cup competitions and was non-playing captain in 1953. He won the British Matchplay Championship three times, as well as many European Championships, and was one of only three players to be made an Honorary Member of the Royal and Ancient Golf Club at St. Andrews. In the early 1950s he was coach to several public schools and through this became a founder member of the Golf Foundation. He did much to raise the standard of play for all professionals in Britain and thought that the "great part of the attraction of golf was its resemblance to life, with a player facing unexpected dangers and dealing with unfortunate situations as they arise".

Henry Cotton was often sought after as an after-dinner speaker both in Britain and abroad, being able to speak French, Spanish and Portuguese. He also worked as a golf architect and wrote many books about the game. Having finally retired to Penina in Portugal, he built a golf course there. Very belatedly he was knighted shortly before his death in 1988.

SAM SNEAD

Sam Snead was born in Virginia in 1912. He was Open Champion in 1946, Masters Champion in 1949, 1952 and 1954, American PGA Champion in 1942, 1949 and 1951 and played in the Ryder Cup in 1937, 1947, 1949, 1951, 1953, 1955 and 1959, acting as non-playing captain in 1969. He never won the United States Open but came very close a few times. He did win eighty-four American tournaments, the highest number achieved by any golfer. Snead still attends the Masters and usually tees off first in the par 3 competition, though he said that 1991 will be his last year.

BEN HOGAN

Born in 1912, Ben Hogan is a living legend, who recently had an exhibition devoted to his life and achievements by the USGA Museum. He was 27 before he turned professional and he won his first major title, the USPGA, in 1946, a victory he repeated in 1948.

In 1949 he had a serious motor accident in which he fractured his pelvis, collar-bone, ankle and rib. Although his career was assumed to have ended, Hogan's sheer determination brought him back into the game after only one year; and a film was made about his recovery entitled *Follow the Sun*, with Glenn Ford. In 1953 Hogan played in just five tournaments and won them

SAM SNEAD
PROFESSIONAL GOLF STAR

Trophies won by Hector Thomson, one of the best amateurs of his time: silver salver, Western Isles Open Golf champion; plated cup on three golf clubs; silver cup on three golf clubs; two tankards, Red Cross Exhibition Golf 1941; mounted Dunlop ball, final round 1936.

Hector Thomson medals. Boxes (left to right): gold medal Glasgow Golf Championship, 1933, Tennant Cup; gold medal Scottish Amateur Championship, 1935; gold medal Amateur Golf Championship, 1936; gold medal Glasgow Golf Championship, 1935, Williamwood Golf Club, Pollack course; gold medal Boy International, 1931, Glasgow. Second row: silver medal, Scottish Amateur Championship; USGA competitor's badge, Amateur Championship, 1936; watch belonging to Jim Ferrier, opponent in 1936; bronze medal, Boy International, 1931, England versus Scotland; bronze medal, Amateur Golf Championship; bronze medal, Amateur Golf Championship; base plaque reading "Presented to Mr. Hector Thomson by the members of the Williamwood Golf Club on his winning the British Amateur Championship on 30th May 1936"; Mountbatten Cup medals, 1930, 1931, and 1932.

Left: Hector Thompson with the Amateur Trophy, 1936.

Middle: Hector Thompson at the age of 3.

Right: Hector Thompson being presented with the Amateur Trophy, 1936.

all. Three of the five were major titles: the Masters in a record of 274, which has only been bettered by Jack Nicklaus with 271 in 1965 and Raymond Floyd also with 271 in 1976; the US Open and the British Open.

Ben Hogan retired in 1968 at the age of 56. In 1965 a poll of US golf writers and sports editors named him the greatest golfer of all time.

HECTOR THOMSON

One of the greatest amateur golfers of his day, Hector Thomson was born in Machnihanish, Argyll, in 1913. His father was a professional golfer and introduced Hector to the game when he was three. After several successes as a junior player, he won the Tennant Cup at the age of 19 and went on to gain the Amateur Championship gold medal in 1936. Hector Thomson turned professional in the 1930s and from 1953 onwards concentrated on teaching in various parts of the world, from Cairo to St Moritz. He was official trainer to the German Ladies National team from 1963–68.

GOLFING FASHIONS

When golf was first played there was no specified mode of dress for the game. This led to a great variety of clothes being worn, especially by gentlemen. The titled gentry were dressed very differently from the working man. In the early days, when the feathery ball was costly, only the rich had the means and the leisure to play. Gentlemen then wore silk top hats, full morning coats in different colours and tight trousers. Caddies, by contrast, were poorly clad in cast-off clothes and with no footwear. Many of the early club portraits of captains that now hang in clubhouses show them wearing top hats and the red coats that were often used so that the golfers could be clearly seen from a distance. The early shoes most probably did not have studs. In this respect the ordinary player gained an advantage, since as a "worker" he would have had his own hob-nailed boots to wear. In addition he usually wore a tam o'shanter, an ordinary shirt with a collar or tie and rough cloth trousers held up with string – a great contrast to the more wealthy.

As the game grew and developed, the less well-off took it up in greater numbers. Clothes etiquette became more varied. Since golf was traditionally regarded as Scottish, many adopted the dress code of the Scots, with knee-breeches, long socks, shoes or boots and a coat giving more freedom around the shoulders to swing the club. In good weather, many golfers put on cricket attire, although generally speaking ordinary suits with top hats continued in fashion.

THE STORY OF A
GOLFING SUIT by
H. Hamilton Fyfe,
from *Golf*, 22 June
1894

Yes, I am a ruined man – "stone-broke," as a slangy friend of mine persists in calling my condition. And what is the cause? Alas! I cannot speak it in any high-sounding phrases full of a comfortable vagueness.

If a man can attribute his bankruptcy to the depreciation in the value of land, or to the general financial depression, he at once gains in esteem and respectability all that he loses in ready cash. People look upon him with reverential compassion as an erstwhile millionaire, or as one who has fallen out of the possession of broad lands, inherited from long lines of prehistoric ancestry. I acknowledge with shame that I owe my fall to a meaner agent. It is a solemn fact that my bankruptcy has been caused by the purchase of a golfing suit.

It was a suit, though! The pattern was to all other patterns ever seen even as a rainbow to a badly-set palette. The cut of the Norfolk jacket – of the knickerbockers – of the cap, which fitly crowned this triumph of tailoring, and was thrown in for nothing – was perfection. Little did I think, as I swaggered complacently down to the station on the first Saturday after the tailor had sent it home, what havoc that suit would make of my life.

When I got to the booking-office I quite intended to take a third-class ticket, according to my usual custom. Indeed, the request for a third-class ticket was on my lips. Whether it was a sudden thought of the incongruity between my appearance and my request, or the unusually respectful attitude and demeanour of the clerk as he leant forward to attend to me, which made me change my mind, I cannot tell. In a lordly tone I demanded a first-class ticket – "Just for this once!" I told myself – and walked down the platform, feeling at least two inches taller . . .

There happened to be playing at the club that day an individual whose claims to distinction were two-fold. He was a famous golfer, and he was a lord; not a peer, but the younger son of one, with a high-sounding courtesy title. It must have been the suit which made this golfing lord show a gracious preference for my society; at any rate, during a foursome in which we were partners, he confided to me in outspoken terms, and in not very good taste, his opinion of the other members of the club, whose guest he was. "Now, look here," he said, "why don't you join the Reedmere Club? – easily the best anywhere near London in every way, ground and membership and everything. You come up and play one day next week, and then if you like I'll put you up. There'll be a committee meeting in about a fortnight." Of course I accepted his invitation, and in due time I was elected a member of the Reedmore Club, "proposed by Lord Tee-Shot, seconded by the Hon. Malcolm MacStimie." A few days after my election the demand for my first year's subscription arrived. I

Opposite: "The Stymie", after a painting by J. C. Dolman, RI, from *Golfing*, December 1934.

Fashion plate for men's Norfolk jackets, *c.* 1910.

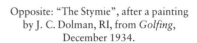

Vie Parisienne cover, 1 June 1929.

Advertisement for James W. Bell Sons and
Co., gentlemen tailors, *c.* 1930.

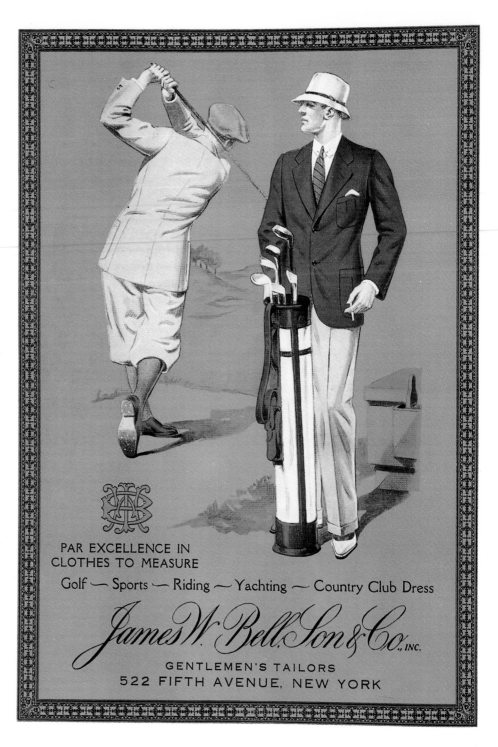

PAR EXCELLENCE IN
CLOTHES TO MEASURE

Golf — Sports — Riding — Yachting — Country Club Dress

James W. Bell Son & Co., INC.

GENTLEMEN'S TAILORS
522 FIFTH AVENUE, NEW YORK

made out a cheque for the, to me, enormous sum required, and sorrowfully reflected
that strict economy during the rest of the year would be necessary if my annual
budget was to be made to show a surplus and not a deficit. I had only played there
twice, however, before I came to the conclusion that my clubs were not quite up to
the mark. I bought the finest set that – er – credit could procure. They were duly
noticed and approved by my aristocratic acquaintances.

But I was becoming reckless. I had now a reputation to keep up. It would never do
to appear in all the splendour of my golfing suit on Saturdays, and to continue to
wear my well-worn raiment all the rest of the week. In six weeks I spent more – I
should say that I obtained on credit – more clothes than I had worn out during all

the rest of my life. Then, of course, there are many incidental expenses which must be incurred by a man who is well dressed – and I flatter myself that, during my brief period of "going it," that description was not undeserved by me.

But by this time my stock of ready-money was almost exhausted. I could no longer afford to lunch at fashionable restaurants. I could no longer indulge in cab-rides. I had not even the price of an omnibus-fare to spare. In fact I had sunk so low that when my creditors became alarmed and writs began to pour in, I was almost happy to be able to appear once again in my true colours.

It is needless to say that I am no longer a member of the Reedmere, or of any other Golf Club. My aristocratic friends have dropped me like a hot potato: my old friends look at me reproachfully. I have given up my chambers, thrown away my chances at the bar (of being able in the course of about ten years or so to make a few hundreds a year), and have taken my passage for India.

It only remains for me to add that the following advertisement has appeared in the newspapers, so far without result:–

"TO BE SOLD. – A second-hand golfing suit; worn very little. A sacrifice. No reasonable offer refused."

The next major change came when tailors created the knickbocker suit, a forerunner to present-day plus-fours, which was first worn by Harry Vardon. Having already enjoyed some popularity among the shooting fraternity, these shortened trousers were now adapted for golf. Knickerbocker plus-fours were cut with an extra four inches of cloth below the length of standard sporting breeches to provide extra movement for the swing. Harold Hilton favoured them, as did Gene Sarazen, George Duncan, Walter Hagen who was a fashion pace-setter, and John Ball. Today they are still worn by Roger Davis and Payne Stewart, who is famous for his colourful selection of plus-fours and sports various different American college colours under contract at the range of tournaments. In summer flannels are now the general norm, and are worn with blazers or club sweaters displaying their own crests. Red coats continue to be worn occasionally, but only at the official functions and dinners held by the older clubs.

Many of today's players advertise makers' names or merchandise on their visors, hats, shirts and sweaters. Nick Faldo has worn Pringle clothes for many years. Altogether golfing fashion today is much more relaxed.

Since women began playing golf in earnest at the end of the nineteenth century, golfing fashions for the ladies have undergone many changes and adaptations. In the early 1890s if a lady swung a club higher than her shoulder, she encountered her large-brimmed hat, a full-length dress with long full sleeves, two full-length petticoats, combinations and, of course, her tightly laced corset. This was the usual dress for ladies and, considering the obstacle it presented, it seems amazing that they succeeded in going any further than the putting green.

Although Mrs Amelia Bloomer had created the split skirt or bloomers as early as the 1840s, very few ladies went as far as wearing them for golf.

Photograph of Bobby Jones wearing plus-fours and leaning on his club, *c.* 1928.

97

Breeches had been adopted for bicycling, but again ladies shunned their use on the fairways. Some women did wear long belted jackets and slightly flared skirts, which appeared more masculine.

The bustles of the 1870s, the flowing designs of the 1880s and 1890s were all easier on a full swing but it remained difficult to avoid revealing the ankle, a form of behaviour that was still considered immoral. Corsets were still a great hindrance, with their twenty-eight whalebones moulded to pinch in the waist and curve out below and above it.

Long skirts caused problems in the wind and especially on wet grass, but the ladies persevered and in 1893 a "New Forest" skirt became the fashion for golf. The length could be adjusted by means of a special tuck with buttons from 12 inches from the ground for golf to 3 inches off the ground for walking home. This skirt also had a removable piece of leather around the bottom edge which could be replaced by a dry cloth edging when entering the clubhouse. A Miss Higgins devised the idea of wearing a wide piece of elastic around the waist which could be dropped to the knees when the wind blew.

Billowing sleeves were either pinned back or tied with elastic. Sailor-type broad-brim hats were pinned to the hair by attractive golfing hat pins made of gold, silver, mother-of-pearl and semi-precious stones. Hats could also be secured with ribbons, elastic or chiffon scarves tied under the chin. Even on the golf course, no lady of any standing would be seen in public without a hat, both to protect her from the sun and to keep her head warm.

Selection of four silver match strikers, 1908–15.

Left: Penrtyn Stanlaws, picture of lady golfer in period dress, *c.* 1905.

Right: Earl Christy, print of the Golfing Girl, *c.* 1905.

Many players wear red coats with their club facings and buttons, and these always look smart. Among them, and one which is quite the neatest of all club uniforms, is that of the Wimbledon Ladies' Club – a coat, with black collar and cuffs, outlined with a piping of white, the buttons being of black, with the club initials in white on them. All clubs that have the privilege of calling themselves Royal are entitled to facings of Royal blue. The Littlestone ladies wear rather a smart coat with white facings, round which are the narrowest of narrow pipings in tri-coloured silk cord, of the club colours, white, green and salmon pink. Green facings are very popular, and are used by the St. Anne's Ladies, the Mid-Surrey and many others. Perhaps the only club with a membership of several hundred, which has no distinctive coat is Princes, at Mitcham, but the charming mixture of chocolate and light blue, in the form of hat ribbons and ties worn by the members, makes rather a welcome change.

By the turn of the century advertisements were appearing for specially adapted corsets and knickberbockers. The Patent Shapely Skirt Association designed a pleated divided skirt which was sold for three guineas. Women golfers were also advised to wear shorter skirts, though these had to be made of tweed or serge so as not to lift in the wind. As hems rose, so footwear became important, but only well-made plain boots were recommended. Studs or nails were advocated in order to help the feet grip the ground but were not suitable for ordinary walking. Gloves were usually worn and made of soft chamois leather, although in some cases old kid gloves were reused.

GOLF from *Sportswoman's Library* ed. Frances E. Slaughter, 1898

Left: J.V. McFall, lady golfer with caddie, 1903.

Right: Chromolithographic calendar for Eusebe Therrien Wine Company, New Bedford, Massachusetts, *c.* 1910.

DRESS by Miss May
Hezlet, from *Ladies'
Golf*, 1904

The time is past when it was thought necessary for the girl or woman who indulged in athletics to make a perfect fright of herself, and to try to imitate men as much as possible; and it has been discovered that there is no advantage to be gained by so doing, that it does not make sport easier, but only attracts much undesirable attention. The "new woman" and the "athletic woman" are no longer subjects for the comic papers to make jests upon, and the majority of girls endeavour to combine comfort and grace, and do not give up all thought of appearance when indulging in their sports. Up to quite recently any old clothes were considered good enough for games, no matter how ugly or unfashionable, and the question of sporting dress received little or no consideration; but now all is changed, and the girl who is wise will take as much trouble over her golf costume as over any other part of her wardrobe.

The question of dress is therefore an important one. One thing which it is absolutely imperative a girl should wear who goes in for athletics is a short skirt. Nothing looks more untidy or unsuitable for games than a long skirt – the hem gets drabbled in mud, or else the wearer is absolutely worn out with the effort of keeping it off the ground. In wet weather the long skirt hampers every movement; it gets soaked with the moisture off the grass, and in consequence becomes a considerable weight, and is very tiring to drag about. A short skirt – really short, not simply a couple of inches off the ground – looks infinitely nicer and more workman-like, and makes an inestimable difference in comfort. The skirt should be well cut, and of some good plain thick stuff, such as tweed or serge, a heavy material for choice, as it does not blow about so much in wind – a flapping skirt is a great nuisance when playing golf, and there are quite enough difficulties to be contended with in bad weather without the addition of an uncomfortable skirt.

With short skirts one must have nice boots, and this item is one for serious consideration, and one which will make a large hole in the average girl's allowance. Cheap boots are no economy; they neither look well nor wear well. A few extra shillings spent at the shop of a thoroughly reliable bootmaker need never be grudged, as it is well-spent money. Good boots keep in shape to the end of their existence, that is, if they are properly looked after and kept on trees while not in use, but cheap boots go out of shape almost immediately, and are always wanting

Opposite: Print of two golfers in period costume, with Cupid holding a bag of clubs, artist unknown, USA, *c.* 1905.

Below left: *The Delineator*, June 1927, Art Deco cover.

Below: Gold and mother-of-pearl umbrella with handle designed as a driver, *c.* 1900.

June 1927   25c

Delineator

A vivid new serial by LOUIS JOSEPH VANCE
"THE WOMAN IN THE SHADOW"
Smart New Fashions

repairs. Brown boots or black are merely a matter of individual choice; brown are usually made of softer leather and perhaps look smarter, but the more unpretentious black wear better in the long run, and are better able to withstand the onslaughts of wet and mud. Waterproof boots can be obtained from most of the good shops, and pigskin or porpoise-hide will be found an excellent material for rough wear. For anyone who plays golf regularly two pairs of thick boots are an absolute necessity, one made extra strong to withstand the wettest grass, and the other of a lighter make to be used in fine weather. The best pattern boots for winter are those lacing half-way up the leg and then buttoning over with flaps, the soles projecting all round. They are undoubtedly heavy, but are a great protection.

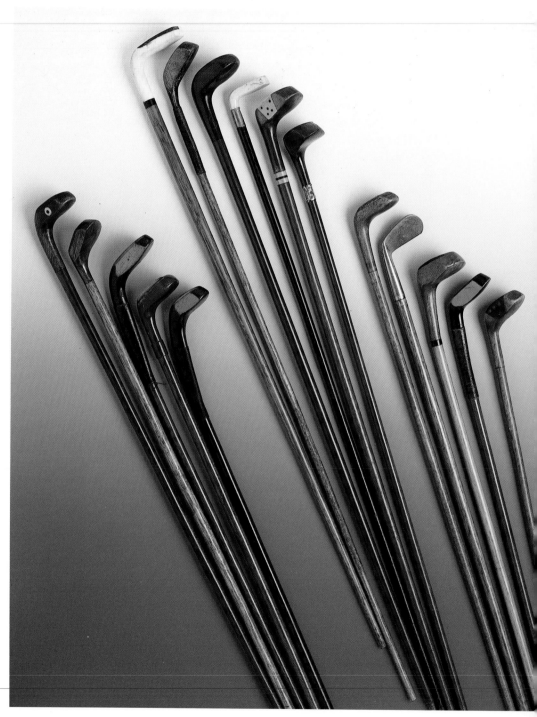

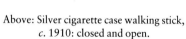

Above: Silver cigarette case walking stick, *c.* 1910: closed and open.

Right: Selection of walking sticks, two ivory *c.* 1900; shaped like long-nose club, drivers and putters, 1900–25.

Photograph hand-painted with oils, golfer unknown, *c.* 1890.

Haynes Salt pottery, "Come rain, come shine", from Denstow's Mother Goose, 13 inches diameter, 1901.

Many people prefer to play in shoes, as they think they have more freedom than in boots, but the drawbacks to shoes are, firstly, that they get filled with sand when walking through bunkers; and, secondly, that the edge of the skirt rubs against the ankles and makes them very wet. The latter contingency, however, can be met by wearing gaiters made of cloth or leather, the leather, perhaps, being the best and most satisfactory for all-round wear. It is hardly necessary to comment on the heels of golfing boots and shoes, which should be broad and flat, as high heels are totally out of place on the links, work havoc on the ground in wet weather, and are very unsafe, as there is always the danger of the wearer spraining her ankle.

In summer weather tennis shoes are often brought into requisition, but tennis shoes are invariably tiring, and increase the size of the feet. One great disadvantage of golf is that it does increase the size of the hands and feet so much. It is an utter impossibility to play well if any restraint is felt in one's clothes, or to walk round the links in tight boots; therefore the muscles which are constantly being exercised have sufficient room to expand, and the consequence is that the more one plays the larger the hands and feet become. Another disadvantage of the game is that being out in all weathers has not a beautifying effect on the complexion. But these disadvantages are minor details not taken into consideration by enthusiasts, to whom fine and bad weather alike are matters of indifference, and who will not be debarred from their pleasure by any outside considerations. The days are past when girls could think of nothing but how best to take care of their complexions, and never by any chance ventured out unprotected in sun or wind. They had, it is true, skins like milk and

roses, and in some ways the change is a pity, as a weather-beaten countenance, to say the least of it, is not attractive; but the new life is a very much healthier one, and sunburn and freckles may have a charm of their own.

As clothes gradually began to be made for comfort and ease of movement in every walk of life, so this more relaxed approach was reflected in golfing wear. Cecil Leitch, British champion of the 1910s and 1920s, had her own very decided views about the subject.

GENERAL ADVICE
TO LADY
PLAYERS by Cecil
Leitch, from *Golf*,
1922

Personal equipment for the game is a matter which is worthy of special attention, not only for appearance's sake, but also for practical reasons.

The majority of lady golfers who attend Championships and other big events are suitably and attractively dressed, but there are some players who handicap themselves by wearing cothes which are not in keeping with the game.

Proper footgear is one of the chief essentials for comfort, efficiency and appearance. Personally I always wear strong shoes with very low square heels and thick soles. High heels are inclined to throw the player forward on to her toes at the top of the swing. This is a very common fault among lady players, and one which must not be encouraged. In addition, high heels are injurious to the course, especially when the ground is soft. I have often been asked whether nails or rubber give the better grip. It is almost impossible to give a definite answer to this question, as so much depends on the nature of ground and weather. Nails which are at all worn are useless on a dry heather course or on a hard-baked inland course during a dry summer, but, on the other hand, rubber can be equally ineffective when the ground is wet. Some players wear rubber tennis shoes when the ground is dry during the summer months, but a heelless shoe is not to be recommended, as it means the player is changing her stance by an inch or more.

In Great Britain there are very few days when tweeds cannot be worn. The summer of 1921 was an exceptionally hot one, but even during the hottest part I

EPNS toasting-fork with "gutty" ball and clubs, *c.* 1910. Asprey golfing set with a score card, original pencil and penknife, *c.* 1925. Silver and tortoise-shell moustache comb made by Samson Mordon, 2½ inches long, 1907. Silver place setting with crossed clubs and ball.

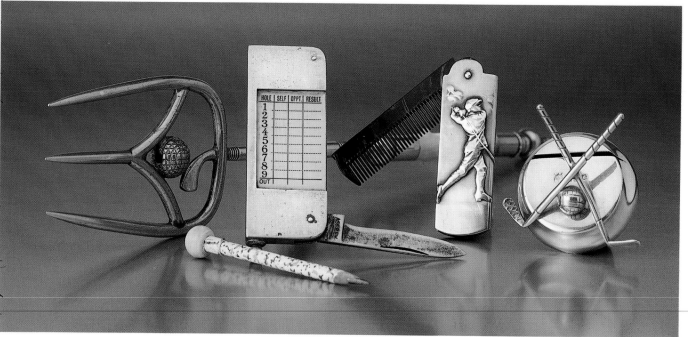

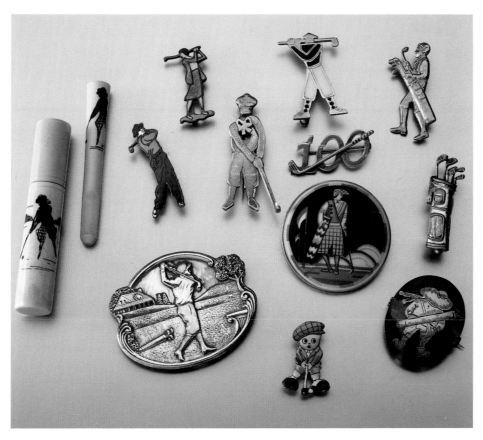

Selection of brooches: lady's cigarette-holder in case, bone and hand-painted sihoute, *c.* 1915; enamel man and woman golfers, *c.* 1930; silver and mother-of-pearl golfer brooch, 1920s; silver brooch in which the arm moves along the "line of the putt", *c.* 1930; "I broke 100" with club, silver, American, 1930s; hand-painted enamel and silver brooch, 1920s; reproduction silver brooch; brass caddie brooch; 1920s; silver bag of clubs, American, *c.* 1940; original Chloe Preston enamel brooch, 1920; silver and tortoise-shell brooch, 1920s.

A cold painted bronze figurine of a caddy boy with ivory head on an onyx base, 8¾ inches high, 1930s.

never found tweeds too heavy. As a matter of fact, I was less affected by the heat when wearing thin tweeds and a cashmere cardigan than the majority of those who wore light skirts and shirts of thin material. Full skirts are to be avoided, but the player must not go to the other extreme. I am often asked if my skirts are cut the exact width of my stance for full shots. They may appear to be so, but this is accident rather than design. Players are inclined to overlook the fact that the width at the bottom of the skirt is not the only part that must receive consideration. It is equally important to allow sufficient width around the knees. For this reason I have all my skirts made from a plain pattern which allows not less than 56 inches around the hem. Pleats about 8 inches wide, back and front, take up this width into the waistband. The ordinary men's tweed materials, which are so admirably suited for golf skirts, are usually about 60 inches wide, in which case a yard and a quarter is sufficient for a skirt and this amount also allows for two patch pockets. Shirt blouses are undoubtedly the neatest and most serviceable for golf, especially the style with which a tie can be worn.

As regards jerseys, nothing looks so neat with a tweed skirt as the plain cardigan style, which buttons down the front and has a pocket on either side.

A suitable hat for golf is a difficult thing to find. My sisters and I have seldom worn hats, and a few years ago we discovered quite by accident a comfortable substitute. This takes the form of an ordinary coloured silk handkerchief folded like a bandage and tied round the head. That there were many players who were looking for such a substitute is proved by the fact that since we first began to wear it hundreds have adopted it.

In cold weather it is almost impossible to keep one's hands warm without some protection. Those players who do not wear gloves when playing will find golfing

A cold painted bronze statue of a lady golfer at the top of her swing, in Art Deco style, on a white onyx base, 11 inches high, 1930s.

mittens a comfort. These should be made of soft wool, and should have a long cuff to go over the jersey cuff. They are quite simple to knit, and when finished resemble an ordinary glove which has had the palm cut out and the fingers and thumbs cut off. An ordinary cuff is knitted and about half the stitches are then cast off; the remaining stitches are then knitted for about an inch and a half, when sufficient must be cast off to allow for the thumb; again the remainder are knitted until a sufficient length to cover the whole of the back of the hand; these are then cast off and loops crocheted for three fingers and thumb. A loop round the forefinger will be found to interfere with the grip. This is the only form of covering for the hands which does not interfere with the grip of those players who do not play in gloves.

While on the subject of gloves it is as well to point out to those who are unable to play without them, the importance of carrying a pair of cotton ones for use in wet weather. The soft chamois leather kind are utterly useless when wet, but a cotton glove affords a better grip the wetter it becomes.

Knitted coats and jumpers soon became the golfers' uniform, with knitted stockings to match, since silk stockings were clearly not suitable. In the 1920s the two-piece knitted twin-set was also popular for golf, although resistance to any kind of trousers for women continued.

By the end of the 1930s divided skirts, often called trouser skirts, were worn by many women golfers, and trousers were made with a small zipped pleat.

After the Second World War Jean Donald Anderson caused an uproar when she played in waterproof trousers in the 1948 Ladies Championship, but by the mid-1950s American women were wearing Burmuda shorts. Today sportswear in general follows changes in fashion from one year to the next and many manufacturers have a large selection of clothes specificlaly for golfers.

In addition to the clothes themselves, a wide variety of accessories have been worn down the decades. Among these are golf scarf pins based on a design consisting of two clubs, one of gold and one of platinum, both aimed at a large golf ball. Another common pin design consists of a silver or gold golf bag containing several clubs. Golf tie clips or holders in enamel with Scottish plaids are also very striking. In the 1920s no really up-to-date golf girl would feel at home on the course unless she wore her shirt fastened with a new gold or silver golf blouse set, which had cuff buttons and studs mounted with embossed golf clubs, either crossed or with a bag.

Decorative score books can be found, bound in morocco and ornamented with a silver Highlander carrying a bag of clubs. Some keen golfers wore a silver chatelaine decorated with the club and bag design. It was also possible to buy umbrella handles with golfing motifs or specially designed silver pieces to be added to the handles of umbrellas and parasols used for golf.

There were silver powder boxes with crossed clubs or a lady golfer on their lids, which were made to hang on the golf girl's chatelaine, together with her tiny silver club case, scissors and golf score cards. Indeed, with so many baubles, it seems fair to wonder whether the ladies really played golf at all.

CHAMPIONSHIPS AND TOURNAMENTS

While the game of golf can be seen as a trial of the individual player's skill, there is no doubt that the major Championship matches offer the best opportunities to see that skill in action. The challenge of playing competitively has brought together the great golfers in every generation and created new heroes for their enthusiastic followers.

THE FIRST AMATEUR CHAMPIONSHIP

The very first Amateur Golf Championship was played at Hoylake in Cheshire in 1885. An entrance fee of one guinea was charged, and prizes were presented by the Royal Liverpool Golf Club. A total of forty-eight entrants took part from various famous clubs. This first Championship was won by a Royal Liverpool golfer, A. F. MacFie, who defeated Horace Hutchinson.

The success of this meeting resulted in the Royal Liverpool Club shortly after suggesting to the Royal and Ancient Golf Club of St. Andrews the institution of an Amateur Golf Championship to be played annually. The idea was received favourably and a number of the leading golf clubs were invited to send delegates to arrange for the playing of the competition. The outcome of a number of meetings was that the present cup was bought by subscription among the invited clubs, regulations were agreed upon and it was decided that the event should be played

Arnold Palmer.

Rare metal badge ticket for the 42nd Open Championship, USGA season ticket 4–11 June 1938, No. 1507, Cherry Hills Club, Denver, Colorado.

HOW ST ANDREWS CAME TO RULE IN BRITAIN by A. C. Fitzherbert, from *Golf Illustrated*, February 1930

Selection of tin badges for various tournaments, 1933–69, including press and guest ticket for the USGA 49th Amateur Golf Championship, 1949, USGA Open Championship, Medinah, Chicago, 1949, Bob Hope Classic, 1969, season ticket for gallery and clubhouse.

yearly at St. Andrews, Hoylake and Prestwick in such order and at such times as the delegates might decide.

In 1922, the Royal and Ancient Club resolved to recognize the Championship of 1885 and to include the winner in their list of champions. The Amateur Championship was played at St. Andrews in 1886, at Hoylake in 1887 and at Prestwick in 1888. Thereafter the Championship was played over these three courses until 1891, when Sandwich was admitted to the list, and the Championship held there in 1892. In the following year, Muirfield was included and the Championship was first played there in 1897. In 1912, the event was played for the first time at Westward Ho!, and in 1923 it was played at Deal.

The old rotation which prevailed from 1892 to 1912 of three Scottish courses and two English courses no longer prevails and there is no no recognized rotation of Championship links used. Originally, twenty-four clubs were associated in the government of the Championship, and in 1914 the Royal Dublin was invited to take part in the control of the games.

These clubs continued to control the management of the Championships until December 1919, when at a meeting in Edinburgh, the Honourable Company of Edinburgh Golfers moved that "believing that in the best interests of the game the time has now arrived when there should be a supreme ruling authority for the management and control of the game; to further this end the Royal and Ancient Golf Club be asked to accept the management of the Amateur Championship and the control of the cup."

There were many thrilling finals at Hoylake. Particularly memorable was the 1902 match. Charles Hutchings was eight up after playing the 6th hole, but owing to his own errors and the deadly pitch-and-run shots played by his opponent Sidney Fry, his advantage dwindled to two up with three to play.

He reached the 16th green in two shots – a notable feat in those days – but was very lazy with his approach putt. Fry, who had put his third shot near the pin, holed out, leaving Hutchings an awkward one for a half. This was the critical point of the match. The putt dropped and everybody breathed again. Refusing to acknowledge defeat, however, Fry won the 17th hole in four. At the last hole his second was away on the right of the green, with his opponent's lying about 8 yards away from the pin. Once more he played a beautiful run up with his "jigger", leaving himself about 4 feet from the hole.

Could the weary Hutchings hole out in two more? Eight yards look like a long distance at the end of a Championship final. Two putts were required for victory. His first putt was very short, but he holed the next amid a mighty burst of cheering from the agonized Hoylake spectators. Thus ended one of the most nerve-racking Royal Liverpool finals, in which Fry's recovery in the

Programmes. (From left to right) official Open Championship programme for 1952, played at Royal Lytham St. Annes, signed on the cover by Peter Thomson, Australia, J. W. Jones and Bobby Locke of South Africa; Illustrated Guide and Hole by Hole Plan of the British Open Championship at St. Andrews, 1955; Charity Golf Match for the British Red Cross Society Sportsman Hospital Fund, Municipal Golf Course, 15 June 1940. Henry Cotton, Richard Burton, Brian Carrick and Leslie Ball all played. Autographed by Henry Cotton.

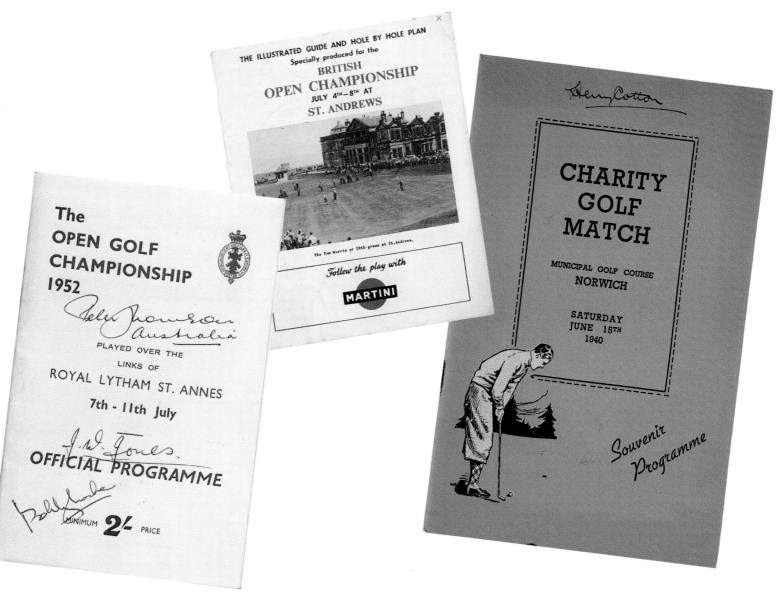

Programme for the 1953 Amateur Championship played at Royal Liverpool Golf Club, Hoylake.

Programme for the opening of the new course at Musselburgh Golf Club at Monkton, 10 May 1938.

BOBBY JONES COMPLETES THE CYCLE by O. B. Keeler, from *American Golfer*, July 1930

last twelve holes must rank as one of the finest ever in Championship golf.

Together with the Open Championship, the United States Open and the United States Amateur, the British Amateur makes up the golfing grand slam, also known as the "impregnable quadrilateral". Only one player, Bobby Jones, has achieved all four titles in one year (1930), although a few have won three, Harold Hilton, Arnold Palmer and Jack Nicklaus among them.

This is written the Sunday morning after the conclusion of the 1930 British Amateur Golf Championship at St Andrews with a brilliant sort of night journey between – these British, perking up of late, had a beautiful special train over the L. N. E. R. at the St Andrews station for those in a hurry to get to London, and, with a considerable party of Americans aboard, it was not unlike a football train home,

119th
OPEN GOLF
CHAMPIONSHIP
ST ANDREWS 1990

R&A MEMBER'S
LADY GUEST

Admit to R&A
Club Tent

DUNLOP MASTERS
TOURNAMENT

Hollinwell Golf Club, Notts
19th, 20th & 21st September 1957

114th
OPEN GOLF
CHAMPIONSHIP
ROYAL ST. GEORGE'S
GOLF CLUB
1985

R & A GUEST

Admit to Clubhouse
and
Club Tent

3rd
EUROPEAN OPEN
WALTON HEATH, LONDON
September, 1980

PRESS STAFF

USI CLASSIC
1972
USI
CLASSIC

GUEST

Pleasant Valley Country Club
958

1974
Season £1.50
CARROLLS
CELEBRATION
INTERNATIONAL

STERS
GE AT ALL TIMES
AUGUSTA NATIONAL GOLF CLUB

012
APRIL
9-10-11-12
CE $50

UNITED STATES
MEDINAH
OPEN CHAMPIONSHIP
1990

00331

MEDIA

Medinah Country Club
June 11-17, 1990 - Medinah Illinois

25th
Anniversary
suntory
WORLD MATCH PLAY
CHAMPIONSHIP

WENTWORTH CLUB 1988

MEMBER

116th OPEN GOLF
CHAMPIONSHIP
MUIRFIELD
1987

GUEST

Admit to Course
NO DOGS
OR CAMERAS

that

DING OF THE

-one Club

ANADA
DRY

3rd
EUROPEAN OPEN
SUNDAY

SPONSORS' STAND

ROW K   SEAT 56

WALTON HEATH, SURREY
SEPTEMBER, 1980

ENTRY TO COURSE
2/6

WEDNESDAY,
15th September, 1937

W/E
R.A.C.
COUNTRY CLUB
CORONATION COURSE
VISITOR

Golf   £3·24

No 1537

To be handed over on request
Available on day of issue only

OPEN
GOLF CHAMPIONSHIP, 1963

ORDINARY
ADMISSION TO COURSE ONLY
FRIDAY, 12th JULY
Charge, 20/-
Available on Day of Issue Only
Not Refundable

No 4062

118th
OPEN GOLF
CHAMPIONSHIP
ROYAL TROON
1989

R & A MEMBER'S
GUEST

Admit to R&A
Club Tent

Selection of tickets for visitors and caddies
to various tournaments, including the
Masters and the British Open
Championship, 1920–88.

when your side has won.

And Bobby had won, at last. I think he was happier over this victory than over any since he broke through with a major triumph in the United States open at Inwood, in 1923. I talked with him a little, immediately after he had been rescued by a squad of big Scottish policemen from some fiteen thousand admirers at the twelfth green, who apparently had determined to take the new champion apart and see what makes him tick so consistently. That is, I talked with Bobby in his room at the hotel; there was no chance to talk to him or to anybody else in the trooping gallery. They had a band at the home green to play him in, but the band got involved in the crowd and I never heard a note sounded.

I asked Bobby:

"Will this success increase your determination to win the British Open also?"

"On the contrary," said Bobby decisively. "I'll do what I can, of course. But I can't

Opposite: Cigarette cards. (From top to
bottom) Tom Morris, No. 33 of 50;
Walker Cup trophy, No. 17 of 25
Sporting Trophies by W. A. and A. C.
Churchman; the Amateur Championship
Cup, No. 16; the Open Golf
Championship Cup, No. 15.

Programme for the 1926 Open Golf
Championship played at Royal Lytham
and St. Anne's.

start breaking my back over anything else for a while. I'm too happy and too
thankful, to have managed to win here."

"Then you regard this as the Big Shot this year?"

"Absolutely! Under the circumstances, this has been the Big Shot for some time.
There could be nothing in golf today that I wanted so much. I can't believe it's really
happened, now."

At which juncture word came that Bobby was to present himself at the Royal and
Ancient club house to receive the cup, on the same little veranda where he stood in
1927 for the presentation of the Open Championship trophy. Apparently convinced
that he was not dreaming, Bobby brushed his tousled hair hastily and went out to
face the huge gallery for the last time.

THE BRITISH OPEN CHAMPIONSHIP

The first Open was played at Prestwick in 1860 and organized by the then club secretary Major J. O. Fairlie. There were only eight players, all professionals. The large leather Championship Belt presented by the Earl of Eglington was first won by Willie Park of Musselburgh. At that time the course was only twelve holes and three rounds were played, all in one day.

The following year amateurs were admitted and the Championship became truly open, although very few amateur players have taken the title, the notable exception being Bobby Jones who won it three times. Apart from 1871 and the war years the Open has been staged every year since. From 1861 to 1870, a period during which Prestwick continued to be the venue for the Championship, Willie Park won a total of three times and Tom Morris four. "Young Tom" Morris was allowed to keep the belt after winning in three consecutive years. Prestwick Golf Club, together with the Royal and Ancient Golf Club and the Honourable Company of Edinburgh Golfers, then subscribed to buy the silver claret jug (of which the champion holds a replica for a year) and a gold medal to be given as a permanent keepsake.

By the turn of the century J. H. Taylor had won his first Open and he, James Braid and Harry Vardon dominated the Championship for the next twenty years. Vardon took six titles and the other two five each. In 1907 Arnaud Massy was the first Frenchman to win, and it was not until 1979 that another European, Severiano Ballesteros, took the title. By then attendance had reached over 134,500 and the total prizes amounted to £155,000. Despite dominating the Open during various periods, including the 1920s and the 1970s, American golfers have almost taken a back seat since 1984.

THE US OPEN

The US Open began in 1894 almost as an afterthought to the US Amateur Championship, the two competitions being staged on consecutive days. By 1900, when Harry Vardon beat J. H. Taylor at Chicago, the US Open had become an international event. Willie Anderson from Scotland won the title four times between 1901 and 1905, with a hat-trick that has never been equalled.

Perhaps the most important early Championship, and certainly one which put golf on the map in America, was held in 1913 at Brookline Country Club, Massachusetts, when 20-year-old former caddie Francis Ouimet beat Vardon and Ted Ray in a play off. Ted Ray later achieved his goal in 1920 and was the last Briton to hold the cup until 1950, when Tony Jacklin won. The year 1920 also saw Bobby Jones play his first US Open as an 18-year-old amateur. On that occasion he tied eighth, although he later went on to win four Opens in eight years.

As the Open became increasingly popular, admission charges were introduced and the prize money was increased. Over the years various players have made their mark at the competition. Ben Hogan won it for the first time in 1948, was unable to defend his title the next year because of his

injuries in a car accident, but came back in 1950 to regain it after a play off. Jack Nicklaus, who as an amateur came second to Arnold Palmer in 1960, turned professional in 1962 and immediately beat Arnie in a play off for the Open, before going on to win eighteen major competitions in the space of nineteen years. Most recently, in 1991, John Daly caused a major upset at Crooked Stick, Indiana, by winning the Championship after starting the week as a ninth alternative.

THE WALKER CUP

As the playing of golf spread through the world, new competitions were created. The Walker Cup began shortly after the end of World War One as a competitition between amateur teams from the United States on the one side, and from Great Britain and Ireland on the other. Although one match was played in 1921, it was in 1922 that George Herbert Walker, who was then president of the USGA, donated the cup which has given the competition its name. Those taking part included Bobby Jones, Francis Ouimet and Chick Evans for the United States, and Cyril Tolley, Roger Wethered and Bernard Darwin for Great Britain. The Americans won by eight matches to four. After two matches in 1923 and 1924, the competition was held biannually until 1938. The Second World War intervened and matches were finally resumed in 1947. Britain has won only three times, in 1938, 1971 and 1989, and drawn once in 1965. The match is played alternately on both sides of the Atlantic at major Championship courses.

Another Walker Cup, more usually known as the J. G. Walker Challenge Cup to avoid confusion, was given to the Championship committee of the Royal and Ancient Golf Club of St Andrews. It is the prize in an annual competition between amateurs representing Scotland and England.

THE RYDER CUP

The Ryder Cup competition developed from an initial match played between representatives of the Professional Golfers Associations of the United States and Great Britain in 1926. Samuel Ryder, who was a seed merchant and gave much of his money to sponsoring golf tournaments, donated the cup from which the competition get its name. He lived in St Albans and was a member of the Verulam Golf Club, where he was captain three times. The cup itself is solid gold and cost £250, then the equivalent of at least $1,000. It was made by Mappin and Webb, and the figure at the top of the cup is of Abe Mitchell, who was to become a personal friend of Sam Ryder and act as his professional at the Verulam Golf Club.

THE RYDER CUP
MATCHES by
Charles Evans, Jr.,
from *Golfers
Magazine*, June
1927

The first strictly official, international match between professional golfers of this country and Great Britain will be played, June 3rd and 4th at Worcester, Massachusetts for a Cup generously presented by Mr. Samuel Ryder.

The American players in this event will all be American born – no naturalized citizen may enter – a distinction never made before, and without doubt, in a way, it will greatly change the character of the event. Heretofore in our matches with Great

Left: Official Souvenir Programme, for the Ryder Cup, 26–27 June 1933 at the Southport and Ainsdale course.

Right: Ryder Cup Official Souvenir Programme, for the Sixth International Match at Southport and Ainsdale Course, 29–30 June 1937.

Britain we have gladly admitted to our teams any good player who had taken the trouble to become a naturalized citizen of the United States, even, perhaps we had welcomed those who were not really naturalized citizens, but had been with us long enough to be identified with our American players.

For years the winners of our National Open were invariably British born, for, of course, there could be no American born golfers of the first rank. It needed something like twenty-five years of golf in America for an American caddie to grow into a first-class American pro., ready to hold his own against the great British players, whether they still played under the British flag, or under the banner of adoption. American boys had to grow up with the game before they were able to cope with British born and British trained players.

The Ryder Cup Matches will be a great competition, and I fancy that the American golfers will not have a walk-over. I am sure that they will take nothing for granted and will fight every step of the way. They may lose even – an unpalatable possibility.

The visiting golfers will also take part in our National Open tournament, which will be played at Pittsburgh June 14–16. Their participation will make, I think, a great difference in this event. Nine expert Britons introduced in any golf event will greatly change its character, and certainly upset many a well-founded expectation.

What they will do to us is problematic. Maybe not so much, and maybe a great deal; but in any case their active presence will add to the interest of our big championship. This is putting it mildly, for it is but simple truth to say that when the leading golfers of America and of Great Britain meet at Pittsburgh the fortunate galleries will be able to view the greatest exhibition of golf in the world. After all professional golf must always average greater than amateur golf, and there on one course will be assembled the greatest professional golfers in the world.

There is not a man who loves the game who is not thrilled at that thought. Who can foretell the outcome of the meeting at Pittsburgh? Will the winner of the team match at Worcester win the National Open? Hardly; Lady Luck is not quite so simple as that. She loves surprises and hands out her own prizes in her own way. The fortunate man, the skilled man, at Worcester, may have grown a little weary and lost a bit of his cunning by the time that he reaches Pittsburgh.

But Worcester comes first: it is only a few days away. And, at the thrilling thought, all that a good sportsman can say is: May the better team win!

"Quiet please" baton used at the British Open Championships.

The British team for the first match was chosen by James Braid, Harry Vardon and John Henry Taylor and included Abe Mitchell (captain), Ted Ray, Fred Robson, George Duncan, Archie Compston, Arthur Havers, George Gadd, Aubrey Borner and Charles Whitecombe. The then editor of *Golf Monthly*, George Philpot, launched an appeal to raise £3,000 to cover their expenses and accompanied the team as manager. At the last minute Abe Mitchell had to withdraw as he had appendicitis, but he later played in the 1929, 1931 and 1933 matches. Ted Ray replaced Abe Mitchell as captain of the 1927 British team, and Walter Hagen acted as captain for the United States. The result was a win for the United States, by 9½ points to 2½.

The year before the first Ryder Cup match, Sam Ryder had set up the Heath and Heather Tournament, the first in Great Britain at which every player was paid £5 and his expenses. This meant that professionals could travel to the match by train and stay overnight without being out of pocket, since their pay for the day was stopped by their own clubs. The prize money was £50 for first place, £25 for second, £15 for third, £10 each for fourth to seventh, £7 10s. each for eight to fifteenth, and £5 each for eighteenth to twentieth. It is interesting to note that the actual Deed of Trust was not drawn up until 8 December 1929, even though the first match had been played on 3–4 June 1927. The deed laid out plans for play by singles on the first day and foursomes on the second, in accordance with the rules of other English Golf Clubs.

Sadly Sam Ryder died from a brain haemorrhage on 2 January 1936. After his death Abe Mitchell became professional at the Verulam Club, having been elected captain of the PGA two years previously. Mitchell died in 1947 at the age of 60.

In 1979 the Ryder Cup was expanded to include European players. Sam Ryder might not have approved, but this move did open up the game considerably. To date there have been twenty-nine matches.

THE CANADA CUP

In 1953 the Canada Cup match was organized for professional players. It later became the World Cup, with participants from all over the world. The winners of the first match were Roberto de Vincenzo and Antonio Cerda, with a combined aggregate of 287. Eight countries competed, and Bobby Locke of South Africa played with Harry Weetman of England.

THE MASTERS

The Masters is an annual competition held at the Augusta National Club in Georgia, the course established by Bobby Jones which was officially opened in January 1933. The first major tournament was played in 1934 and named the Augusta National Invitation Tournament as Bobby Jones did not like the title "The Masters". After much thought, however, Jones relented and in 1938 the name "Masters" was officially adopted.

Competing at the Masters is by invitation only. The first winner in 1934 was Horton Smith, and since then some of the more famous names to win have included Jack Nicklaus (six times), Arnold Palmer (four times), Tom Watson (twice), Seve Ballesteros (twice), and Nick Faldo (twice in succes-

Rosette badges given by Harold W. Pierce with Royal and Ancient Golf Club buttons in rosette badges; white for referee, red for members of the Greens Committee, blue for members of the Championship Committee.

MASTERS
28012
SERIES · APRIL
1981 · 9-10-11-12
PRICE $50

1986 · 00228
APRIL 9 WEDNESDAY · PRACTICE ROUND
PAR-3 CONTEST
TICKET MUST BE DISPLAYED
00228

08964
1986
MASTERS TOURNAMENT
WEDNESDAY, APRIL 9
NOT GOOD FOR PAR-3 CONTEST
08964

MASTERS
SERIES · APRIL
1974 · 11-12-13-14
21352
PRICE $20

MASTERS
SERIES · APRIL
1969 · 10-11-12-13
5414
PRICE $20

MASTERS
3271
SERIES BADGE 1964

MASTERS
SERIES · APRIL
1978 · 6-7-8-9
14962

MASTERS
SERIES · APRIL
1970 · 9-10-11-12
8274
PRICE $20

MASTERS
1165
SERIES BADGE 1965

MASTERS
SERIES · APRIL
1979 · 12-13-14-15
15933

MASTERS
SERIES · APRIL
1971 · 8-9-10-11
18743
PRICE $25

MASTERS
SERIES · 1966
PRICE $15.00 · 4633

MASTERS
1988 · April 7-10
X16906
PRICE $85

MASTERS
SERIES · APRIL
1977 · 7-8-9-10
27595
PRICE $35

MASTERS
SERIES · APRIL
1967 · 6-7-8-9
14339
PRICE $20

MASTERS
1989 · April 6-9
A08244
PRICE $90

MASTERS
SERIES · APRIL
1972 · 6-7-8-9

MASTERS
SERIES · APRIL
1968 · 11-12-13-14
PRICE $20

sion). Of these only Nicklaus has successfully defended his title in consecutive years, and nobody has managed to win three times in a row. Nicklaus also set the course record of 271 in 1965, although this was matched in 1976 by Ray Floyd.

LYLE'S NAIL-BITING FINISH WINS MASTERS BY 1 SHOT by David Westin, from the *Augusta Chronicle*, 11 April 1988

Displaying coolness under fire not seen at Augusta National since Arnold Palmer in 1960, Scotland's Sandy Lyle used a brilliant birdie on the final hole to win the 52nd Masters on Sunday.

Not since Palmer's victory 28 years ago had a golfer won the Masters in such dramatic fashion – making a birdie on the final hole of regulation while playing in the final group of the day.

With Mark Calcavecchia waiting in the wings, Lyle needed a par on no. 18 to assure a play off. Calcavecchia, playing in the group ahead of Lyle, had scrambled to par the hole for a 2-under-par 70.

Lyle's drive on the par 4 hole found the front left fairway bunker, more than 140 yards from the pin. Playing in his seventh Masters, Lyle could see victory slipping away as he took his stance in the shifting sand.

"I personally thought it was over," said the first Scotsman to win the Masters. "That front bunker has a steep face. The place I didn't want to hit it was in the front, lefthand bunker. I didn't think I'd have a chance of getting it out of that bunker and getting it to the green."

The long-hitting Lyle lofted a magnificent 7 iron to about 30 feet above the hole. The gallery cheered as it slowly trickled down the slope, resting 10 feet from victory.

A selection of Masters tickets from 1964 to 1989 and a Par 3 competition ticket for 1986.

"I was lucky it was up the face (in the bunker) and I had a good lie and I had enough club to get it there," Lyle said.

The 10-foot birdie putt awaiting him had no break, "but it's not a putt you want to have every day of the week," he said. "Anybody in that position, for what it is worth and the honour of winning that tournament, you're not going to feel that confident. Your knees are knocking a little bit. You've been there so many times, like in play off conditions. You've got to go through the motion. I've learned to keep my nerves under reasonable control."

Lyle kept his nerves in check, but stunned Calcavecchia as he rolled in the birdie for his second major Championship.

"I'm still a little bit stunned," said Calcavecchia. "I didn't think he would make birdie on the hole from where he was and under those circumstances. It would have been pretty easy to make bogey."

The 11th, 12th and 13th holes at Augusta are known collectively as Amen Corner, and it is here that the Masters Tournament can be won or lost. The 15th par 5 with water surrounding the green needs nerves of steel to carry to a successful conclusion. It is this hole that Jack Nicklaus made his eagle, and here that Seve Ballesteros hit his into the water, when it seemed he had won!

The 1991 Masters was the fifty-fifth competition with a purse of $1.3 million. The format is 72 holes with 18 each day in stroke play. After 36 holes, the leading forty-four players and all those tied for forty-fourth place, plus all within ten strokes of the lead, qualify for the final two rounds. If there is a tie, the match is decided by a sudden death play off.

An "Allround" Player

Left: The trophy for the World Amateur Golf Council, founded 1958. The inscription reads, "To foster friendship and sportsmanship among the people of the world".

Right: USGA Amateur Championship medal, 2–9 September 1922 at Brookline, Massachusetts. The winner was J. Sweetser, 3 and 2.

THE WORLD AMATEUR TEAM CHAMPIONSHIPS

A plan for a World Amateur Team Championship was conceived by the USGA and presented to the Royal and Ancient Golf Club at St Andrews in March 1958. A joint conference created the World Amateur Golf Council, with thirty-two organizations to conduct the Championship. What began as a proposal for a women's match in 1964 between the United States and France grew into the Women's World Amateur Team Championship.

SENIOR GOLFERS

Senior golfers have competed in Professional Golf Association Seniors Championships since 1937. However, it was not until 1978, when Jimmy Demaret organized the Legends of Golf Tournament at Onion Creek Golf Club, that senior golf caught the public eye. The fifty-four ball competition attracted twenty-eight of golf's all-time great players and the inaugural event was won by the team of Sam Snead and Gardner Dickinson.

The popularity of the Legends Tournament led to a meeting in January 1980 at which the groundwork was laid for the Senior PGA Tour. Sam Snead, Gardner Dickinson, Bob Goalby, Don January and Dan Sikes were appointed to the Senior Advisory Council. In the same year the PGA Tour ran two senior events, and the USGA held their first Seniors Open, which was won by Roberto de Vincenzo at Winged Foot Golf Club.

The Senior PGA Tour was regarded by many people as the most successful professional sports venture of the 1980s, and now features over forty events each year. Golfers of the Seniors Tour delight and entertain the galleries. More than just colourful personalities, they are talented and determined competitors. The success of the Seniors Tour and the skill of the players confirm that golf is, indeed, the game of a lifetime. In order to qualify a player has to have reached the age of 50. Jack Nicklaus joined in 1990 and won in his first year!

THE CURTIS CUP

The Curtis Cup was donated by Margaret and Harriet Curtis to stimulate friendly rivalry among the women golfers of many lands. In 1932 the series began with a match between the lady golfers of the United States and those representing Great Britain and Ireland.

The long awaited and much heralded official International golf matches, between the women of the United States and those of Great Britain, will be inaugurated in 1932. The good news was recently released by H. H. Ramsey, President of the United States Golf Association, who, through his efforts to bring about these matches, has added another chapter to his already long list of golf achievements, which we hope will live forever, and that's a long time.

THE CURTIS CUP MATCHES by Virginia Holzderber, from *Golfers Magazine*, July 1931

Glenna Collett of Providence, American Lady champion, from *Golf Monthly*, 1922.

The Curtis Cup, which, of course, ultimately will take its place in the Hall of Sport Fame directly alongside her big brothers, The America's Cup, The Davis Cup and The Walker Cup, has been donated by Margaret and Harriet Curtis, of Boston, both of whom have been prominent and active, not only as players of the game but in the advancement of its popularity among women. It is most agreeable and women golfers are fortunate to have their generous wholehearted support in this movement, that will do much more than simply advance the interest in golf, among women, as an international competitive sport.

The direct negotiating for the first matches has been conducted by the Women's Committee of the United States Golf Association and a Committee of the Ladies' Golf Union of Great Britain, all of whom are eminently qualified for the task at hand. It is natural to suppose the mechanics of team selection and play will be patterned somewhat after the manner of the Walker Cup matches. The first match in 1932 will be played in England and a match every two years thereafter alternating between the United States and Great Britain, regardless of which country might be in possession of the cup.

The donors of the Curtis Cup and the others, wish I could name them all here, who have worked untiringly to bring about these regular International Team Matches, have done more than provide an opportunity for good sport. They have made possible a real step toward that "World Peace" we hear so much about. Show me a man interested in clean sport and you will find in him a man honest in his

Above: The Men's Amateur Trophy, the USGA Haveneyer trophy for the National Amateur Championship, was presented to the USGA by Edward Moore in 1895. First won by Charles Blair McDonald in 1895, later in 1903 by Walter Travis, 1911 Harold Hilton, 1924, 1925, 1928 and 1929 Bobby Jones, 1954 Arnold Palmer, 1959 Jack Nicklaus, 1970 Lanny Watkins, 1973 Craig Stadler.

Right: Badges: Marshall for 33rd National Golf Championship, 1929; President USGA, Amateur Championship Souvenir, Chicago Golf Club, 1887; golf USGA official press, Maury Fitzgerald.

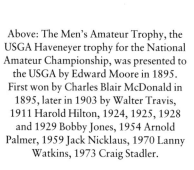

122

business dealings, fair in his judgement of men and tolerant of the fellow trying. This is equally true as between nations, and after all, I think of a nation as nothing more than a lot of children grown up.

Women have a lot to say about things that shall or shall not happen in this world of ours today and we have not had the advantage of much in the way of international contact, but with all things there must be a beginning, and these Curtis Cup matches will afford every woman golfer an opportunity to do her bit. Make these Curtis Cup matches a great success for the love of the sport and the opportunity they will afford for a closer woman's international relationship.

THE USGA

The United States Golf Association was formed on 22 December 1894 after two clubs proclaimed different United States Amateur Champions. While the original charter was formed by only five clubs, today there are over 5,500 member clubs and courses. In 1895 the USGA organized three Championships – the Amateur, the Open and the Women's Amateur – and today it runs a total of thirteen Championships, the presiding three and the Women's Open, the Senior Open, the Amateur Public Links, the Women's Public Links, the Junior Amateur, the Girls' Junior, the Senior Women's Amateur, the Senior Amateur, the Mid-Amateur and the Women's Mid-Amateur.

HOW PALMER WON THE US OPEN by Joe E. Doan, from *Golf Monthly*, August 1960

If you had scanned the scoreboard at Cherry Hills in Denver, Colorado, site of the Open, after the third round, you would have sworn that Palmer didn't have a chance. Thirteen names preceded his and he was seven strokes off the 208-pace that burly Mike Souchak was pursuing. Sandwiched between Souchak and Palmer were such redoubtables as Dow Finsterwald and Julius Boros with 210, Jack Nicklaus (211), Ben Hogan (211), Gary Player (213), Bill Casper Jr. and Sam Snead (both 214).

To that point, Palmer had played consistently, but not brilliantly. His scores were 72-71-72. His total of 143 at the midway point had left him eight strokes behind Souchak and in a tie for 15th place with six others. Souchak's 135, by the way, was the lowest halfway total ever recorded, three strokes under the old mark.

When Palmer started the final round most of the gallery of 15,000 or so were elsewhere. On the first hole he hit an electrifying tee shot to the green 346 yards away. His putt from 20 feet rolled to within a foot of the cup, but he almost missed the tap-in. But nobody got very excited about that "birdie", not even Palmer.

Badges: USGA Committee badges for President 1895 and 1896, Executive Committee 1899, Committee member E. Meister Junior 1889; Official Press M. S. Druchenbrod; Executive Committee.

But it started a rash of one-under-par efforts and by the time Arnold played out the 7th hole, he had scored six "birdies". Nothing like it ever had been perpetrated in a previous US Open. He got his "birdie" on the second hole with a 35-foot run-up from off the edge of the green; on no. 3 he hit a wedge to within a foot of the cup and got a third "birdie"; the fourth "birdie" followed on the next hole when he dropped a 20-footer.

A drive into the rough on the long 5th (538 yards) interrupted his sub-par spree but he still got down in regulation figures. On the par 3 no. 6, Palmer hit the green, 174 yards from the tee, with a 7 iron and rolled in a downhill 25-putt for a 2. On the 7th he hit a wedge approach to within 6 feet of the cup and got another "birdie". A one-over-par on the 8th hole followed by a par at no. 9 gave him an incredible 30

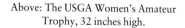

Above: The USGA Women's Amateur Trophy, 32 inches high.

Right: The Lennox Cup, won in 1895 and 1896 by Arthur H. Fenn, presented to the winner by President William McKinley at the Lennox Links, Massachusetts.

going out. News of Arnold's white-hot play travelled the length and breadth of the course and, as he moved on from hole to hole, his following snowballed.

On the incoming nine, however, the galleryites were disappointed if they expected to see the PGA circuit's leading money winner continue his torrid pace. Palmer played a kind of holding action game on the second nine, getting only one "birdie" but making sure that eight solid pars were in his collection. He got a 35 coming in for a 65, the lowest final round ever shot by a US Open winner.

The USGA also sponsors the four international amateur events, Walker Cup Match for gentlemen, the Curtis Cup matches for ladies and the World Amateur Team Championships for ladies and gentlemen. Thirty-eight committees of more than seven hundred volunteers look after every aspect of the game.

COLLECTING GOLFIANA

P eople with an interest in golf need not confine themselves to playing the game and retiring to the nineteenth hole for a shot-by-shot discussion of what has happened on the greens. Golf is steeped in history and offers a wealth of different fields to the collector. None need be expensive, although obviously the older the item, the more costly it is likely to be. It is always best to consult a specialist dealer, especially as there are now a number of reproductions on the market which are very good and sometimes difficult to detect from the originals.

One obvious area in which to collect is that of equipment. The hickory-shafted pre-1935 clubs with good cleek marks and putters are popular. Since displaying clubs takes up a lot of room it may be advisable to choose one maker and only collect a small number. Golf balls are plentiful and occupy less space. Ideally they should be in good condition, if possible still wrapped and boxed. Even modern logo balls are fun. The World Hall of Fame in Pinehurst has over 2,500 on display.

Golfing literature comes under many headings: historical, biographical, instructional, architectural, and so on. Book collectors may prefer to decide on one particular area that appeals most to them. The field is large, but browsing through bookshops brings great pleasure.

Horses' shoes. These leather boots were also used for horses in about 1900. The fairways were protected and the horses had a sure footing on the inclines.

O'Hara dial pitcher, 6½ inch, *c.* 1910.

O'Hara dial pitcher, rear view.

Lenox hand-painted three-handled toasting mug with silver rim, *c.* 1902.

There is no doubt that golf book collecting is growing in popularity. Many among the world's millions of golfers collect and cherish good books, and what is more natural than that they should set aside a corner of their library for their favourite recreation? Although from the general world standpoint, golf is only some sixty years old, quite five hundred books have been published during that period. But the early books are getting scarce, and the collector with an eye to the future is buying these and first editions as soon as he can before they disappear from the market altogether.

Naturally, golf's first books were published in Scotland, unless you are a believer in the theory that the game descended from the Dutch "Kolven," in which case your literary field will be extended to the early 1700s. "Des Menschen. Begin, Midden en Einde" ("The Beginning, Middle and End of Man"), by J. Luiken, was published in Amsterdam in 1712, and contains an illustration purported to be a golfer. Some collectors, however, disregard these Dutch books.

Most of the early British items were poems, the best known being Thomas Mathison's "The Goff," published in Edinburgh in 1743 at four pence, and now worth something in the region of fifty dollars. Other early books were G. F. Carnegie's "Golfiana," privately printed in 1833; "Carminum Rariorum Macaroni-cum Delectus," 1813; "The Golfer's Manual," by "A Keen Hand" (H. B. Farnie), giving a historical and descriptive account of golf, published in 1857; Charles MacArthur's "Golfers' Annual," 1869; Chambers' "Few Rambling Remarks on

GOLF BOOK
COLLECTING by
H. E. Worden, from
Golf Illustrated,
June 1934

Rare 1907 calendar for MacNiven and Cameron's Pens, with picture entitled "On the Links".

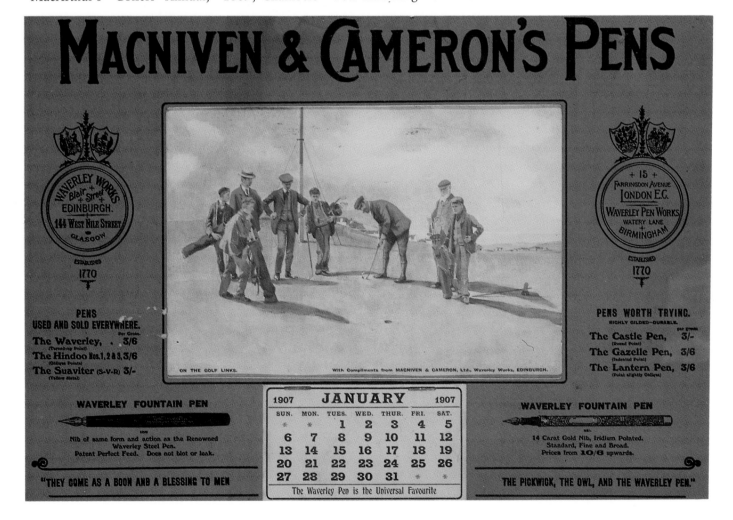

A Lenox mug by the Ceramic Art Company, 5½ inches tall, *c.* 1900. This was hand-painted. Lenoxware is almost like porcelain and highly sought after.

A Lenox mug with sterling silver rim by the Ceramic Art Company, 6 inches tall, *c.* 1900. Only a few selected pieces had silver added.

Most of these golfing scenes were manufactured for a very short time between 1894 and 1906.

Golf," 1862, and Robb's "Historical Gossip about Golf and Golfers," 1863.

It was not, however, until the printing in 1875 of Robert Clark's "Golf: A Royal and Ancient Game" that the really literary field was entered, and so well produced was this book that it has remained the criterion ever since. It contained practically everything that could be found of historic interest – poems, songs, extracts from club minutes, private diaries, Acts of Parliament, so that in the preface to a second edition in 1893 the author expressed disappointment to find that the first edition had exhausted nearly all that had been written about the game. It was issued to subscribers only, and there was also a limited large paper edition, numbered from 1 to 50 with extra plates. The latter are nearly all in private collections, but there are a few of the ordinary edition about which realize from five to six dollars, besides many copies of the cheaper re-issues of 1893, 1899 and 1900.

The next "milestone" was "The Art of Golf," by Sir Walter G. Simpson, Bart., 1887, which with Horace Hutchinson's "Hints on Golf," 1886, was the first drop in the present-day flood of instructional books. This was priced at one shilling and ran into some fifteen editions, and now only the first is scarce. Simpson's book, a more sumptuous work, still fetches near the published figure of fifteen shillings ($3.75), and this is becoming scarce.

From Stobart and Son (specialists in golf books and prints), of London, England, I am advised that other sought after books of this period are James Lindsay Stewart's "Golfiana Miscellanea," a collection of interesting monographs, 1887; Thomas Marsh's "Blackheath Golfing Lays," privately printed in 1873; "Lays of the Links – A Score of Parodies," anonymous, but written by T. Ross Stewart, 1895; John Thompson's "Golfing and Other Poems and Songs," 1893 (with large paper edition,

50 copies); "Poems on Golf," collected by members of the Edinbugh Burgess Golfing Society, privately printed, 1867.

The next book of importance – probably a big factor in popularizing the game – was the Badminton Library volume on golf, edited by Horace G. Hutchinson in 1890, which ran into a great number of editions, and the ubiquitous brown covers of which are to be found on most booksellers' shelves. The large paper edition (limited to 250 copies) is scarce.

The Reverend John Kerr's "Golf Book of East Lothian," small and large paper editions of 500 and 250 copies respectively, was another scholarly volume, appearing in 1896, and contains over 500 pages, quarto size. It contains an enormous amount of information of some of the oldest clubs in the world. Other "club records" of historic value are: W. E. Hughes's "Chronicles of the Blackheath

From left to right: Edward VIII Duke of Windsor; Turf cigarette card showing Henry Cotton, No. 1 of 50; Mill hof and Co. cigarette card, No. 8 of series of 36 entitled 'In the Public Eye', James Braid.

A selection of covers from *The American Golfer*, 1922–25.

Golfers," 1897, and H. S. C. Everard's: "History of the Royal and Ancient Golf Club, St. Andrews," in 1907.

"The Golfing Annual" was begun in London in 1888, and was issued for 23 years; a complete set is worth acquiring, as it contains not only lists of clubs and full records but interesting articles and verses by the writers of the day. "Golf," a weekly journal, was commenced September 1890, and ran until June 1899, when it was merged into "Golf Illustrated," which then started No. 1. The 18 volumes of "Golf" constitute a unique record; complete sets are not common.

One of the first books to be published in the United States was James P. Lee's "Golf in America," 1895, followed in 1897 by H. J. Whigham's "How to Play Golf," in which action photos were first used to illustrate the text. Since then many splendid volumes have appeared, notably Charles Blair Macdonald's "Scotland's Gift: Golf," constituting a history of the game, particularly in America.

Above: Original poster for Arthur Bell
and Sons Old Scotch Whisky, Perth,
Scotland, 30 × 22 inches, *c.* 1900.

Left: Rare Johnny Walker tin calendar
with golfer and caddie, *c.* 1910.

Opposite above: Tom Browne, *The Caddies Get the Price of a Bottle of Whisky*, pen and ink drawing, *c.* 1900.

Opposite below: A selection of Crown Ducal pottery, 1920s–1930s. The cigarette box measures 7 × 3 inches and the vase is 9 inches high. The plate with the floral surround is in the Horentine series.

OLD PRINTS AS CLUB DECORATIONS by Edward Wenham, from *Golf Illustrated*, February 1930

Left: Wedgewood Etruria series. England No. 2632. The Golfer is Cyril Tolley. 10 inches diameter, 1932.

Right: Wedgewood and Sons Burslem Sports Series. Designed by Arthur Dale Holland and Kennard Wedgewood in 1931, this was lightly printed in outline and finely hand-painted by Dale Holland. Pearlware by Kennard Wedgewood. Only about twenty-five were made in 1931.

Ephemera such as postcards, scorecards, greetings cards, programmes, autographs and brochures should be within most collectors' pocket. Silver spoons, trophies, match safes, pencils and so on are more costly, but may have additional historical interest, especially if engraved with the name of a great golfer.

Ceramics are very attractive and can be bracketed together with original paintings and prints as most were hand-painted. Even the new signed limited-edition prints should not be rejected, since they may well become tomorrow's antiques.

Possibly, of all the portraits of golfers, the one conveying the most aristocratic mien is that of James Ashton, painted by Frederick Reynolds. Complete in periwig and cravat, with ruffles covering his dainty wrists, this old player stands serene in the complacency afforded by his own perfection. One wonders whether the kneeling figure of the caddie is representative of homage, or whether the boy is simply collecting the clubs. Also, one wonders, whether the player succeeds in retaining his wig, when accosted by some of those high winds, which furnish our excuses for "slices" and "pulls."

These and other reproductions of old pictures, connected with golf, will always retain their interest to followers of the Royal and Ancient Game. The fact that they elicit the attention of members and visitors is in itself proof of their historical interest, although, perhaps, portraits do not make so general an appeal as do pictures representative of events in the golfing world of early times.

Undoubtedly, the picture of this latter type, which has the most artistic beauty, is that of Mary, Queen of Scotland, playing at St. Andrews in 1563. The queen is attended by Chastelard and it is interesting to recall that Chastelard, during the stay

at the famous golfing town, rose to favor, but presuming upon this, was, within a few months, beheaded in the old market place.

There is much in pictorial golf, which would signify that the game attained considerable popularity among royal personages of the Tudor and Stuart periods. One instance is that of King Charles the First, playing at Leith, near Edinburgh, when news was received of the rebellion in Ireland. Of St. Andrews and the matches, which have been played there in its early history, several pictures are obtainable.

Always remember that what goes up can as easily come down in price. If you like an item, then buy it. The joy is in building a collection and the friends you make from all over the world in the process. There is now hardly a country that does not play golf or want to know about the game's history. Collecting golfiana is fascinating and time-consuming but the rewards are very high. The illustrations in this book and in *Golf: The Golden Years* give some indication of the range of artefacts available. In 1970 the Golf Collectors Society, PO Box 491, Shawnee Mission, Kansas 66201, was formed for the interchange of information about collecting. The society holds regular meetings throughout the United States and a national meeting in the autumn.

GENE SARAZEN AND THE WILSON TECHNICAL STAFF AT WORK IN THE GOLF CLUB FACTORY—WILSON-WESTERN SPORTING GOODS CO. CHICAGO

BRASSEY GOLF NOTES

At this little game there is not the least doubt You have to be BRASSEY You're nothing without.

Golf has grown to be so large a feature of modern Anglo-Saxon life as to be almost ubiquitous. It is difficult to escape it; and even the ground of Art is not too sacred for its intrusion. We have actually seen Golf treated dramatically – *pour rire*, as by Mr. Arthur Roberts, or incidentally, as by Mr. Barrie, if we mistake not. Elsewhere the golfer may have appeared on the stage and escaped our notice: it is only a wonder that we have not had more of him. He has not left music quite alone, golfing songs have been many in number. Mercifully, he has not yet invaded the sphere of operatic music, though the notion of his invasion suggests great possibilities – of tender treatment, as he addresses himself to the short putt with a *smorzando* movement, followed by the *finale furioso* when the put is missed. And thoughout the action the dreadful stimy motive, suggested or realized, might recur hauntingly – the idea is not copyright! It would be a hard thing to say, after so much has been written about him, that he plays no part at all in literary art; yet the hard saying is very nearly the true one. We know of no golfer, as such, artistically portrayed, unless it be perhaps in that old story from the *Contes du Roi Cambrinus*, named *Le Grand Choleur*, of

THE GOLFER IN ART by H. G. Hutchinson, from *Golf*, 17 January 1896

Opposite: Silver and enamel match striker.

Opposite left: Gene Sarazen and staff at work at the Wilson-Western Sporting Goods Co. factory, 1933.

Opposite right: Golf Notes, 'Brassey', chromolithograph, 1903.

W. Wood and Co. hand-painted biscuit barrel, 6 inches to top of handle, *c.* 1915, Staffordshire. The golf ball gives an idea of the size.

Moon plate made by Wedgewood and Sons, England, 1972.

A golf dining chair with needlepoint cover. Note golf ball and clubs.

which Miss Bruce once published a translation in *Longman's Magazine*. And, after all, *chole* is not Golf, though possibly a lineal ancestor. The great Golf novel, like the great American novel, has yet to be written, and we may confess to a secret doubt whether, even then, it will be read.

But there is one art – an older and more primitive art than any of these, probably – in which the golfer has figured often, and figures more and more frequently as he becomes more popular – the limner's art. We find him in many of the pictures of the old Dutch artists, a familiar figure to Van der Veyde and to Van de Neer. (We know that Holland was an old home of Golf – possibly even its nursery – for does not a protectionist Act of the Scottish Parliament forbid the importation of Dutch-made Golf balls?) In most of the Dutch pictures the golfer is portrayed playing on the ice. But this is not always the case, and in a small drawing of an interior, by Rembrandt we believe, a glimpse through the open door shows us the figure of a golfer playing before the house. Earlier than the time of these Dutchmen, however, we find the golfer depicted occasionally in old missals. That which is prefixed to Mr. Andrew Lang's historical introduction to the game in the Badminton Library book is an instance; though in the case of this particular illustration it is not impossible for the sceptical critic to suggest that the game might equally well be hockey. It may be that the designer suffered under a similar confusion of ideas about the two games to that which possessed many Englishmen until about a decade ago. But there exists another missal, which the indefatigable Mr. Lang routed out of the British Museum comparatively lately, in which Golf, almost exactly as we know it, is, beyond all question, the game portrayed. Curiously enough one of the performers seems to be kneeling down to putt, and it looks as if one of his opponents, moved to just indignation, were expostulating with him on such a gross breach of golfing etiquette, though on what rule of present-day Golf he could convict him we are rather at a loss to know. For the most part, these old Dutchmen, and the rest of them, are not

Left and right: Postcards.

Above: The golfing caddie is 5 inches high and is a rare companion figure to the golfer.

Opposite: A selection of Carlton Ware by Wiltshaw and Robinson, Stoke-on-Trent, dating from 1910–40. The cereal dish is an unusual pattern and measures 7½ inches in diameter, the hot water jug is 6 inches tall and shows the golfing scene usual for this manufacturer. The humidor can come in various colours and measures 5½ inches.

playing with any very dashing driving. Of course, they suffered under the inestimable disadvantage of living before the days of the Badminton book. All allowance is to be made for them. Still it is singular that few of the rather grotesque figures portrayed on the Dutch tiles and elsewhere, seem to have got much beyond the half-swing. Certainly, this seems to show want of enterprise on their part, which may be taken as a significant coincidence with the decadence of their naval strength. Of the pictures that survive to us of Golf since it made its home in Scotland, it is very noticeable that few of them depict the golfer in the act of making the stroke. Most of the artists seem confined by the classic tradition, and portray rest in preference to movement. Charles I is receiving the news of the Irish rebellion on the Leith links,

"Caddie Sir?"

but he is breaking off his game to read the letter. Modern golfing manners would disapprove of such disturbing intelligence being imparted in the course of the game. The messenger should have waited till it was over. Many other pictures are familiar to us – the gentleman with his club over his shoulder, with the three-corner-hatted caddie behind, and no lack of a subtle humour in the lines of either face. Then there is he with the epaulettes and Golf clubs, and many others; but in none of them do we see the swing depicted. The man was the picture, not the style.

There is indeed one most animated picture, in which action is everywhere – that picture of putting out at the old Ginger-beer Hole at St. Andrews, wherein players and spectators are crowding forward, more irrepressibly than even a St. Andrews gallery of to-day, and endeavouring by all manner of excited gesture to affect the laws of dynamics by which the ball is taken towards the hole. But even there the stroke has been already played, the ball has left the club, and the volition of the player has no more influence over it; even this short putt we are not allowed to see in course of execution.

In the United States the USGA acts as custodian of golfing history and has both a museum and an extensive library at Far Hills, New Jersey. The museum exhibits include clubs and balls, paintings, sculptures, ceramics, glassware, trophies and silver pieces; and over the last thirty years all champions have been encouraged to donate both the clubs they won with and their completed scorecards.

Royal Doulton Bunnykins Milk Jug. 7 inches high.

Opposite: Leigh Kidman, *"Caddie, sir?"*, watercolour, 1930.

Hand-painted wine glass with golf ball, *c.* 1950. Hole in one trophy with a Warwick 4 ball, *c.* 1950. Advertising calendar with Penfold ball, *c.* 1930.

Greetings cards. (From left to right): Bob Hope ; Valentine's Day card, chromolithograph by John Winsch, 1911; "The game of golf, your honour", Christmas card, 1900; Charles Crombie, "With all good wishes", Christmas card, 1907; "Everybody's Doing It", Christmas card, 1914.

Below: Ungar silver top with crystal glass base from dressing-table set, *c*. 1910, USA. EPNS inkstand with a glass insert, a mesh-type ball as the base and crossed iron clubs to hold a pen. An amber and amethyst stone is used to represent the golf ball, *c*. 1910. Silver blotter, marked 925 silver, most probably Continental, *c*. 1910.

Let others sing of Summer's smiles,
  Of courses baked as hard as brick
On which our tee-shots run for miles,
  Although our pitches will not stick.
    I find I get a bigger kick
Out of the joys of winter play;
  Unless the fog is extra thick,
I like a round on Christmas Day.

Let others plead for "winter rules"
  And leave to tee up through the green;
That is the cry of modern schools,
  Who cannot take their divots clean.
    I take my iron – and quinine* –
To get my second shots away
  Unless the frost is extra keen
I like a round on Christmas Day.

Just one preliminary swig –
  Slow back, old man, and swallow through –
And I don't care a blasted fig
  For any gale that ever blew.
    And though at times I drive askew,
And put my pitch-shots far astray,
  Unless the fairways are like glue,
I like a round on Christmas Day.

Of course, I play the Nineteenth twice –
  Both going out and coming in.
I've always found it good advice:
  A spot of whisky or of gin,
  Will help our putts to reach the tin,
And keep rheumatic chills away;
  I'm all for "hitting past the chin";
I like a round on Christmas Day.

A SONG OF
CHRISTMAS GOLF
by Hari-Kari, from
Golfing, December
1935

* *With acknowledgments to "Candid Caddies."*

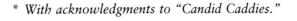

GOLF COLLECTIBLE SHOPS

Sarah Fabian Baddiel
Golf Gallery
Grays-in-the-Mews B10
Grays Antique Market
Davies Mews
London W1
tel. 071-408-1239

Old St. Andrews Golf Gallery
6 Golf Place
St. Andrews
Scotland
tel. 0334-77840

Colonel J. C. Furniss
Crossway House
Torthorwald
Dumfries DG1 3PT
Scotland
tel. 0387-75624

Burlington Galleries
12 Burlington Gardens
London W1X 1LG
tel. 071-734-9984

Grant Books
Victoria Square
Droitwich WR9 8DE
tel. 0905-778155

McEwan Fine Books
Ballater
Aberdeenshire AB3 5UB
Scotland
tel. 0338-55429

Morton W. Olman
325 West 5th Street
Cincinnati
Ohio 45202
USA
tel. 513-241-7797

Bob Gowland
Oscroft Restorations
The Sandhouse
Waste Lane
Kelshall
Turporley CW6 0PE
tel. 0829-51268
(reproduction and repairs of clubs)

Golf's Golden Years
2929 N. Western Avenue
Chicago
Illinois 60618
USA
tel. 708-934-4108

George and Susan Lewis
P.O. Box 291
Mamaroneck
New York 10543
USA
tel. 914-698-4579

Richard Donovan
PO Box 7070
305 Massachusetts Avenue
Endicott
New York 13760
USA
tel. 607-786-0883

Leo M. Kelly
6244 Beechwood Road
Matteson
Illinois 60443
USA
tel. 708-729-0046

Bob Pringle
49 Ayr Street
Troon
Ayrshire KA10 6EB
Scotland
tel. 0292-311822

BIBLIOGRAPHY

Henderson, Ian, and Stirk, David, *Golf in the Making*, 1979.
Olamn, John M. and Morton W., *The Encyclopedia of Golf*, 1985.
Watt, Alick A., *Collecting Old Golf Clubs*, 1985.

MUSEUMS TO VISIT

British Golf Museum
St. Andrews
Fife KY16 9JD
Scotland
tel. 0334-72423

Archie Baird's Golf Museum
Gullane Golf Club
Gullane
East Lothian
Scotland
tel. 087-57-277

USGA Golf House
Far Hills
New York 07931
USA
tel. 908-234-2300

World Golf Hall of Fame and Museum
PGA Boulevard PO Box 1908
Pinehurst
North Carolina 28374
USA
tel. 919-295-6651

Ralph W. Millar Library and Museum
Industry Hills Golf Club
California 91744
USA
tel. 818-854-2354

British Columbia Golf Museum
2545 Blanca Street
Vancouver
British Columbia V6R 4N1
Canada
tel. 604-222-GOLF

AUCTION HOUSES

Phillips
New House
150 Christleton Road
Chester
Cheshire CH3 5TD
tel. 0244-313936

Sothebys
35 Bond Street
London W1

Christie's Scotland Ltd
164–166 Bath Street
Glasgow G2 4TG
Scotland
tel. 041-332-8134

Sporting Antiquities
47 Leonard Road
Melrose
Massachusetts 02176
USA
tel. 617-662-6588

Richard Olivers Auction Gallery
Route 1 Plaza 1 PO Box 337
Kennebunk
Maine 04043
USA
tel. 207-985-3600

INDEX

Page numbers in *italic* refer to captions and illustrations